Federalism in Taxation

AEI STUDIES IN REGULATION AND FEDERALISM
Christopher C. DeMuth and Jonathan R. Macey, series editors

FEDERALISM IN TAXATION: THE CASE FOR GREATER UNIFORMITY
Daniel Shaviro

PRODUCT-RISK LABELING: A FEDERAL RESPONSIBILITY
W. Kip Viscusi

STATE AND FEDERAL REGULATION OF NATIONAL ADVERTISING
J. Howard Beales and Timothy J. Muris

WORST OF BOTH WORLDS? STATE RATE REGULATION AND
ANTITRUST EXEMPTION IN INSURANCE MARKETS
Jonathan R. Macey and Geoffrey P. Miller

Federalism in Taxation

The Case for
Greater Uniformity

Daniel Shaviro

The AEI Press

Publisher for the American Enterprise Institute
WASHINGTON, D.C.

1993

Distributed by arrangement with

UPA, Inc.
4720 Boston Way   3 Henrietta Street
Lanham, Md. 20706   London WC2E 8LU England

Library of Congress Cataloging-in-Publication Data

Shaviro, Daniel N.
    Federalism in taxation : the case for greater uniformity /
Daniel Shaviro.
    p.   cm. — (AEI studies)
    Includes bibliographical references.
    ISBN 0-8447-3823-9. — ISBN 0-8447-3822-0 (pbk.)
    1. Intergovernmental tax relations—United States.   2. Fiscal
policy—United States.   3. Taxation—Law and legislation—United
States.   4. Interstate commerce—Taxation—United States.
I. Title.   II. Series.
HJ275.S49   1993
336.2'00973—dc20   92-37929
                                                             CIP

1 3 5 7 9 10 8 6 4 2

THE AEI PRESS
Publisher for the American Enterprise Institute
1150 17th Street, N.W., Washington, D.C. 20036

Printed in the United States of America

Contents

CONTENTS

Foreword

DANIEL SHAVIRO's study of local, state, and federal taxation is one of a series of research monographs commissioned by the American Enterprise Institute's Regulation and Federalism Project. The purpose of the project is to examine the advantages and disadvantages of American federalism in important areas of contemporary business regulation, including product labeling, advertising, insurance, transportation, communications, and environmental quality.

The benefits of state autonomy—diversity, responsiveness to local circumstances, and constraint on the power of the national government—are fundamental to the American political creed and deeply embedded in our political institutions. Are these benefits real and substantial in the case of business regulation? How do they compare with the costs of duplication, inconsistency, and interference with free interstate commerce that state regulation can entail? Has the growth of national and international commerce altered the balance of federalism's benefits and costs—for example, by affecting the ability of individual states to pursue local policies at the expense of citizens of other states? Are there practical means of reducing the economic costs of state autonomy in regulation while preserving its political benefits?

The authors of these volumes have found different answers to these questions in the context of different markets and regulatory regimes: they call for greater national uniformity in some cases, greater state autonomy in others, and a revision of the rules of state "policy competition" in still others. We hope that this research will be useful to officials and legislators at all levels of government and to the business executives who must live with their policies. More generally, we hope that the AEI project will prove to be a significant contribution to our understanding of one of the most distinctive and important features of American government.

Each of the monographs produced for the Regulation and Federalism Project was discussed and criticized at an AEI seminar involving federal and state lawmakers, business executives, professionals, and academic experts with a wide range of interests and viewpoints. I would like to thank all of them for their contributions, noting, however, that final exposition and conclusions were entirely the work of the authors of each monograph. I am particularly grateful to Jonathan R. Macey of Cornell University and Heather Gradison of AEI, who organized and directed the project's research and seminars along with me, and to John D. Ong and Jon V. Heider of the BFGoodrich Company and Patricia H. Engman of the Business Roundtable, who suggested the project in the first place, worked hard and effectively to raise financial support for it, and provided valuable counsel and encouragement throughout.

CHRISTOPHER C. DeMUTH
President, American Enterprise Institute
for Public Policy Research

1

Introduction

OVER THE PAST THIRTY YEARS, state and local tax receipts have more than doubled in real terms and have even increased relative to U.S. government tax receipts and gross national product.[1] They now account for more than $400 billion annually, or more than 30 percent of the taxes collected in this country and 10 percent of gross national product.[2] Over the next few years, state and local taxation may continue to increase in importance, since expansion of government services seems more likely to occur below the national level and since, for political reasons, the taxing authority is often the same as the spending authority.[3]

As a result, the interaction between taxation and federalism is more important than ever. What are the consequences of assigning to limited geographical jurisdictions, subject to congressional and federal judicial review, so much of the power to levy and collect taxes that inevitably have national effects? Given the danger of protectionist or burden-exporting local legislation, as well as the overlap with national taxation—in tension with the maxim of federalism that generally only one level of government should regulate any subject—one might expect the existing practice of federalism in taxation to have attracted widespread criticism.[4] Yet the literature has proved

---

[1]On the growth in state and local tax receipts, see Jerome Hellerstein and Walter Hellerstein, *State and Local Taxation: Cases and Materials*, 5th ed. (St. Paul, Minn.: West Publishing Co., 1988), pp. 5, 9. On their growth relative to U.S. government tax receipts and gross national product, see Joseph Pechman, *Federal Tax Policy*, 5th ed. (Washington, D.C.: Brookings Institution, 1987), p. 3.

[2]See Pechman, pp. 2–3.

[3]From 1980 through at least 1987, state and local governments' share of total government expenditures in this country increased. See Richard A. Musgrave and Peggy B. Musgrave, *Public Finance in Theory and Practice*, 5th ed. (New York: McGraw-Hill, 1989), p. 476.

[4]See, for example, Edmund Kitch, "Regulation and the American Common Mar-

1

surprisingly favorable to current practice. The conventional viewpoint, rooted in deference to our historical traditions, goes something as follows:[5]

While the state and local exercise of taxing power has costs given the danger of discrimination against interstate commerce and the incentive to export the burden of state and local taxation to outsiders, these costs can be kept relatively modest. States gain from reciprocal forbearance, market forces impede tax exporting, and states face constitutional constraints under the commerce, due process, and equal protection clauses.[6] The remaining costs imposed are plausibly offset by the advantages of local control, such as interstate tax competition, smaller government units' increased responsiveness to voters,[7] and voters' ability to exercise the "exit option."[8]

I think this answer is too optimistic and is in some respects wrong. First, "discrimination" is too narrow a conception of how state and local taxation can distort or impair national markets. Even if no jurisdiction targets interstate commerce for unfavorable treatment, disparities in state and local taxation have many of the same effects on business and personal decision making as an outright tariff at the jurisdictional boundary. The problem in both cases is one of loca-

---

ket," in *Regulation, Federalism, and Interstate Commerce*, ed. A. Dan Tarlock (Cambridge, Mass.: Gelgeschlager, Gunn, & Hain, 1980), p. 47.

[5]See, for example, Walter Hellerstein, "State Income Taxation of Multi-jurisdictional Corporations: Reflections on Mobil, Exxon, and H.R. 5076, *Michigan Law Review* 79 (1980): 113, 160: "Absent some pressing need for federal intervention . . . the states should be free to go their own way. Our constitutional system contemplates concurrent state and federal taxation, with considerable latitude accorded to the states in this domain."

[6]See, for example, Charles McLure, "Tax Exporting and the Commerce Clause," in *Fiscal Federalism and the Taxation of Natural Resources*, ed. Charles McLure and Peter Mieszkowski (Cambridge, Mass.: Lincoln Institute of Land Policy, 1983), p. 169.

[7]See, for example, Michael McConnell, "Federalism: Evaluating the Founders' Design," *University of Chicago Law Review* 54 (1987): 1484, 1493.

[8]The seminal work on the exit option's relevance to local government is Charles Tiebout, "A Pure Theory of Local Expenditures," *Journal of Political Economy* 64 (1956): 416.

tional nonneutrality, due to tax rules. Second, the attempt to limit discrimination, as distinct from requiring locational neutrality, is inherently complicated and costly, especially if left to the courts.[9] Third, political forces, such as reciprocal forbearance, operating at the state and local level cannot always be counted on to limit locational distortion, even when no discrimination is deliberately intended. In particular, even if political decision making is no worse at the state and local level than at the national level, the administrative and compliance costs imposed by seemingly trivial variations between tax systems present powerful grounds for desiring greater uniformity. Fourth, the belief of state and local governments or voters that they can export tax burdens to outsiders need not be factually correct to have adverse consequences. Fifth, in the tax area, the benefits of increasing governmental responsiveness by placing authority at the state and local level seem overrated. These benefits are less significant especially when the issue is how to define a tax base, rather than how much revenue to raise through taxes of one sort or another.

While constitutional and political constraints, along with the better counterarguments in favor of state and local government taxing authority, defeat an unambiguous "right answer," we should move toward confining states' taxing authority to the determination of their tax rates, not the precise contours of the tax bases to which they apply these rates. Thus, I urge that Congress encourage or require the states to use partly or wholly uniform tax bases for business and perhaps personal income taxes, to make greater use of tax credits and uniform allocation rules where taxpayers have a multijurisdictional presence, and when levying taxes that seem directed principally at outsiders, such as excise and severance taxes on oil and coal, to use rates no higher than those applying to comparable in-state levies. Such legislation would almost surely be within Congress's broad commerce clause powers. But, given that for 200 years Congress has almost never used these powers to constrain state and local discretion over taxes,[10] the enactment of such legislation may

---

[9]This is not to say that the logical endpoint of a locational neutrality standard, requiring all states and localities to levy precisely the same taxes at the same rates, would be either good policy or a constitutionally defensible position for a court. See chapter 4, the section entitled "Preserving Broad State and Local Autonomy."

[10]Congress did not first exercise its powers to restrict state and local taxation of

3

be unlikely. In the absence of congressional action, the courts should more consistently and coherently bar discrimination against interstate commerce and attempted tax exportation and should attach less weight to the countervailing concern for state and local government autonomy.

My arguments might support stronger limitations than the above. By keeping my proposals relatively modest, however, I aim to stay unambiguously where the costs of decentralization continue to exceed the benefits significantly. Complete centralization of authority over taxation, while having significant advantages, would on balance be undesirable. My primary point is not that federalism in taxation is wholly misconceived, or that state and local governments have no valuable role to play, but that the balance is askew.

Unfortunately, while we ought to be moving toward greater uniformity—and while the European Community, often viewed as a major trade rival of the United States, is doing precisely that—we are currently moving in the opposite direction.[11] The Supreme Court is entering an era of wholesale retreat from even its limited past efforts in the area. Congress gives no indication of taking over the Court's coordinating role, and the state governments' increasing revenue pressures may limit their willingness to cooperate even where it is in their collective long-term interest. Perhaps in the long run, as the costs of Balkanization become both greater and more apparent (particularly in contrast with the European example), the arguments I present will gain influence.

Chapter 2 of this volume examines the reasons for preferring locationally neutral taxes and explains the basic tension between locational neutrality and state and local autonomy in taxation. Chapter 3 examines the federal judicial check on state and local taxation, which often relies on a principle barring discrimination against

---

interstate commerce until 1959. Hellerstein and Hellerstein, *State and Local Taxation*, p. 324. It has continued to exercise such power only rarely. Walter Hellerstein, "State Taxation of Interstate Business: Perspectives on Two Centuries of Constitutional Adjudication," *Tax Lawyer* 41 (1987): 37.

[11]See, for example, David R. Cameron, "The 1992 Initiative: Causes and Consequences," in *Euro-Politics: Institutions and Policy-Making in the "New" European Community*, ed. Alberta M. Spragia (Washington, D.C.: Brookings Institution, 1992), describing the continuing evolution of an increasingly integrated internal market within the European Community.

outsiders or interstate commerce. Chapter 4 explores the need for a broad federal judicial check by examining state and local governments' reasons for imposing or avoiding locationally distortive taxes, the countervailing benefits of allowing such governments broad autonomy in taxation, and Congress's willingness to strike down locationally distortive taxes under its commerce clause powers. Chapter 5, the conclusion, provides specific recommendations for congressional and judicial action or alternatively for legal change by state governments that appreciate the advantages of greater uniformity.

2
Tariffs, Taxes, and Locational Neutrality

To BEGIN, I will examine the potential problems created by state and local taxation.

The Harms to Be Avoided

The capacity of state and local taxation to burden national markets has long been recognized. Indeed, the paradigmatic form of burden—protectionist tariffs on the passage of goods across state boundaries—provided one of the chief motives for the Constitutional Convention in 1787.[1] In explaining why protectionist tariffs were undesirable, the framers principally stressed the enmity resulting from states' competition to tax and disfavor each other.[2] Yet they also recognized, at least roughly, a second type of harm caused by tariffs: adverse wealth effects or inefficiency. This harm results from reducing aggregate social gains from trade and, on a locational basis, distorting economic decisions and substituting high-cost for low-cost production.[3] These two types of harm continue to be recognized today as the main grounds for aversion to state and local governmental tariffs,[4] as

[1] See *Federalist* No. 7, pp. 62–63, and No. 42, pp. 267–68 (all references to *The Federalist* are to the New American Library edition, edited by Clinton Rossiter, 1961); and Sholley, "The Negative Implications of the Commerce Clause," *University of Chicago Law Review* 3 (1936): 556, 559–60. Interstate commerce issues, despite their importance to the calling of the Constitutional Convention, mostly dwelt in the background during drafting and ratification.

[2] See *Federalist* No. 7, pp. 62–63, and No. 42, pp. 267–68.

[3] See *Federalist* No. 7, pp. 91–92, describing the benefits of a flourishing and unrestricted commerce.

[4] See, for example, Philip M. Tatarowicz and Rebecca R. Mims-Velarde, "An

well as to taxes that have similar effects even if they do not formally tax the act of crossing a boundary.[5]

As a matter of policy, I focus principally on locational distortion, because at present enmity between the states is far less important, and locational distortion far more so, than was the case in 1787. Moreover, a conventional ground for emphasizing enmity—the fear that one state's tariffs will provoke retaliatory tariffs by other states, leading inexorably to trade wars—contains a circularity.[6] Unless tariffs are for some independent reason undesirable, what could be wrong with having more of them? The likelihood of retaliation may be relevant in deciding when the federal government should intervene, but it fails to answer the question of what state and local taxes are undesirable in the first place, and why.

The framers, while concerned about retaliatory tariffs, also feared that the enmity between the states arising from taxation would have far broader consequences, including a possibility of armed conflict.[7] This concern was understandable and, at the time, probably realistic. The American Revolution had been prompted in large part by disputes over taxing authority;[8] the classical and recent European

---

Analytical Approach to State Tax Discrimination under the Commerce Clause," *Vanderbilt Law Review* 39 (1986): 879, 882. Donald Regan places great weight on a third objection to tariffs: that they are "inconsistent with the very idea of a political union. . . . the economic equivalent of war. . . . hostile in [their] essence." See Donald Regan, "The Supreme Court and State Protectionism: Making Sense of the Dormant Commerce Clause," *Michigan Law Review* 84 (1986): 1091, 1113. I disregard this objection on the grounds that notional "wars" matter only to the extent that they harm or anger people and that it is unduly difficult to decide which actions, among a variety that are consciously or implicitly self-serving, are impermissibly hostile.

[5]The framers recognized that tariffs were only one means of causing geographical distortion. See *Federalist* No. 7, pp. 62–63, noting that so long as states can pursue commercial policies peculiar to themselves, there will be injurious regulations of trade designed to benefit in-state at the expense of out-of-state residents.

[6]See, for example, Tatarowicz and Mims-Velarde, "An Analytical Approach to State Tax Discrimination," p. 883; Regan, "The Supreme Court and State Protectionism," p. 1114.

[7]See *Federalist* No. 6, pp. 54, 57; No. 7, pp. 62–63; and No. 42, pp. 267–68.

[8]See, for example, Lawrence Gipson, *The Coming of the Revolution 1763–1775* (New York: Harper & Row, 1954), pp. 69–100; Edmund Morgan, *The Birth of the Republic 1763–1789* (Chicago: University of Chicago Press, 1977), pp. 14–27, 42–60.

7

history that the framers studied so carefully revealed that commercial disputes could lead to war; and government power and citizen loyalty were distributed very differently from the way they are today.[9] The state governments were truly sovereign entities with a primary claim on most people's loyalties, which even the framers expected to remain preeminent.[10] This is hardly surprising for an age of relatively low mobility and trade, when travel and communication over geographical expanses were vastly more difficult and expensive than they are now—and when the country was new and the Civil War had not yet been fought. Today actual war between the states is a chimera, the former Soviet Union's or Yugoslavia's problems notwithstanding; even lesser degrees of interstate conflict or rivalry, while perhaps relevant, are a greatly diminished concern.[11]

Even to the extent that enmity or rivalry between the states remains an important problem, it fails to suggest a clear, generalizable standard for identifying objectionable state and local taxes.[12] One's enmity toward others is a product of one's perceptions about them, not necessarily of what they are actually doing, and perceptions cannot easily be measured or predicted. Other than on a case-by-case basis, it would be difficult to identify the class of state and local taxes likely to create excessive enmity.

On the other side of the comparison, the principal argument for attaching such great importance to locational neutrality is one of

---

[9]See *Federalist* No. 6, pp. 57–58.

[10]See, for example, *Federalist* No. 46, pp. 295–300.

[11]While regional loyalties (for example, as a Southerner or New Englander) remain culturally important today, state tax rivalries often involve neighbors from the same region. See, for example, Matter of Speno v. Gallman, 35 N.Y.2d 256 (1974), concerning New York's attempt to tax New Jersey residents who worked in New York.

[12]A standard barring discrimination against interstate commerce, which might be thought to address the perception-of-enmity problem, has difficulties that I discuss in chapter 3. Even if this standard worked better, however, I doubt that an empirical study would reveal much effect on popular perceptions regarding the behavior of other states. Ironically, perhaps the clearest recent example of a tax that created interstate enmity, Wyoming's severance tax on coal, viewed by many as an OPEC-style extraction of monopoly rents by "blue-eyed Arabs," was upheld by the Supreme Court under the antidiscrimination standard. See Commonwealth Edison v. Montana, 453 U.S. 609 (1981); Walter Hellerstein, "Constitutional Limits on State Tax Exportation," *American Bar Foundation Research Journal* (1982): 1.

efficiency. As an economic matter, all else being equal—an important qualification that I will relax later[13]—it is optimal that the tax levied on a given amount of profit or a given taxpayer not vary according to the location of any property or persons.[14] Taxes are generally transfer payments, rather than net costs to society or compensation for the use or consumption of scarce resources. Thus, stylized economic actors making cost-benefit calculations but self-lessly seeking to maximize social rather than personal good would disregard their tax bills in making personal and business decisions. Equally stylized but selfish actors will not disregard their tax bills in making locational decisions, however, unless taxation is constant across different locations. Accordingly, under standard economic assumptions, locational neutrality minimizes the real social costs of production and ensures that low-cost producers will out-compete high-cost but otherwise equivalent producers. Even when personal consumption rather than business decision making is involved, locational neutrality in taxation permits people to maximize their own good, taking account of social costs.[15]

Taxes inevitably have income effects—by reducing taxpayers' wealth, they affect their behavior. But to the extent avoidable, they ought not to have substitution effects. When they cause taxpayers to substitute an activity for the one they would otherwise prefer in order to reduce their tax liability, substitution effects create a dead-weight social loss in the amount of the reduced pretax benefit to the

---

[13]See chapter 4, section entitled "Preserving Broad State and Local Autonomy."

[14]See, for example, Charles McLure, "The State Corporate Income Tax: Lambs in Wolves' Clothing," in *The Economics of Taxation* eds. Henry Aaron and Michael J. Boskin (Washington, D.C.: Brookings Institution, 1980), pp. 327, 345. McLure notes that this insight, while standard in discussion of international taxation, tends to be ignored in discussions of state taxation—a point that is as true now as when McLure made it more than ten years ago.

[15]Locational neutrality may be desirable even if market outcomes are flawed by externalities. Problems with market outcomes merely make possible a second-best defense of locational disparities as an offset to other distortions. Without any good reason for expecting such offset, however, it is common to assume that avoiding further distortions is desirable. See, for example, E. J. Mishan, *Second Thoughts on Second Best*, Oxford Economic Papers no. 14 (Oxford: Clarendon Press, 1962), pp. 205, 214. In addition, locational neutrality within the United States is desirable even if it does not exist worldwide, if only to benefit the doing of business within the United States.

9

taxpayers by reason of the substitution. In the absence of externalities, the conclusion that the substitution is a loss follows logically from assuming that consumers generally know better than legislators, if not absolutely, what is best for themselves.

Locational neutrality is far more important today than in 1787. Today's far greater economic relationships among the states, founded above all on drastic reductions in the costs of travel and communication, suggest a commensurately greater elasticity of response to locational tax disparities. Thus, the efficiency consequences of locational disparities have probably grown significantly.[16] Moreover, the immense real growth in state and local taxation since 1787 would make the problem a larger one even without any other changes. Further, as I will discuss shortly, the notion of state and local tax efficiency involves more than merely comparing the tax burdens in different locations. It is complicated by the question of what benefits the taxpayers receive in return for taxes paid, a trade-off that is more likely to be roughly even and thus not to deter entry if the taxpayers voluntarily choose to pay them, to finance higher spending, in their capacity as voters. Today's more integrated national economy presents greater opportunities than existed in 1787 for states to reach across their borders and tax nonconsenting nonbeneficiaries.

The analysis thus far has depended on incompletely explored assumptions about taxation, going to the efficiency reasons for preferring that taxpayers base decisions on pretax rather than posttax outcomes. Before further discussing locational neutrality and comparing it with a standard barring discrimination against interstate commerce, I will explore more carefully the definitions and assumptions about taxes that qualify the meaning and importance of locational neutrality.

The Definition of a Tax and Its Significance for Locational Neutrality

In common usage, not all laws requiring value to be transferred to governments are taxes. We speak of income, sales, and property

---

[16]In contrast, though, the efficiency consequences of a particular jurisdiction's undesirable taxes and regulations have been reduced, since greater mobility permits disfavored activities to move to other jurisdictions instead of being wholly suppressed.

taxes; business, excise, and severance taxes; gift, estate, and inheritance taxes; and the like. Yet items such as highway tolls, public transit fares, tuition charged by state universities, and fines for criminal behavior are not commonly called taxes. More generally, transfers of value to the government are not called taxes when they have either of two characteristics. First, if paid directly in exchange for specific services, such as a subway ride or a college education, they are called user fees. Second, if levied principally to affect behavior rather than to raise revenue, they are called regulation.[17]

Both distinctions are imprecise. Consider a "car user fee," enacted to replace a substantively identical personal property tax on cars, that directly benefits the payers only in the sense that they avoid penalty for nonpayment and are permitted to drive.[18] Or consider a tax on the rental of hotel rooms—arguably a user fee if it merely defrays the costs that visitors impose on the taxing jurisdiction, but more of a tax as it begins to swell general revenues.[19]

As for the distinction between taxes and regulation, colonial Americans encountered its vagaries when they took the position, in connection with their claim that England could regulate but not tax their trade, that a sixpence duty on foreign molasses was within the power of Parliament because it would end the molasses trade. Cutting the duty in half to three pence, however, so that it was no longer prohibitive and therefore raised revenue, would, they claimed, in-

---

[17]A tax could alternatively be defined as any regulatory provision that imposes costs on private parties, even if the costs are dead-weight social losses rather than transfers. I define taxes more narrowly and distinguish them from regulation, given this volume's purpose of examining the provisions that state and local governments use primarily to raise revenue.

[18]Musgrave and Musgrave, *Public Finance in Theory and Practice*, p. 212, define a user fee as a "voluntary" payment, but this begs the question of whether, for example, an income tax is voluntary because one could avoid it by earning no taxable income.

[19]The hotel example helps to clarify that even what looks like a market exchange involving a government may belong in the tax realm if the government is using its coercive powers to charge a monopoly price. Thus, imagine that the above government repealed its hotel tax but used its eminent domain and police powers to take over all hotels in the jurisdiction and bar any new hotels from entering the local market. The example would be substantively identical to that in the main text if the government then set room prices to equal the "normal" (that is, previous private) charge plus the earlier hotel tax.

fringe the fundamental liberties of English subjects.[20] Even when the substantive distinction between raising revenue and seeking behavioral responses appears clear, common usage is not always consistent with it. Consider a tariff set high enough to keep out all foreign trade, thus raising no revenue. While the provision meets my definition of regulation, it might be called a tax given its form and the likely surreptitiousness of the regulatory motive. Similarly, an income tax rule permitting homeowners to deduct lodging costs against taxable income, thereby understating the consumption component of income for the regulatory purpose of favoring home ownership, is commonly classified as part of the income tax.

While mindful of the murkiness of the distinctions, I define *taxes* for purposes of this volume as provisions that, unlike user fees, are simple transfers to government rather than market-style exchanges of value for specific goods or services, and that, unlike regulation, principally serve revenue-raising objectives. To the extent that a transfer is part of a market-style exchange or serves regulatory objectives, my analysis remains relevant but incomplete. In particular, consider the statement that, from an efficiency standpoint, taxes are costs one would prefer the taxpayer to ignore. Plainly it is not efficient for prospective payers to disregard user fees that reflect the cost of providing them with services.[21] Moreover, if we assume that a particular regulation is a good one, then presumably we do want it to affect people's behavior. Thus, to the extent that a levy imposed by a state or local government is a user fee or regulation, rather than a tax, additional issues are presented—on the user-fee side, concerning whether it may reduce locational or other distortions by making the payers internalize the actual social costs of their presence; and on the regulation side, concerning whether any distortions resulting from the levy might be either desirable in themselves or worth the price of achieving the regulatory aim.[22]

---

[20]See Gipson, *The Coming of the Revolution*, p. 184.

[21]The efficiency issue is more complicated where user fees pay for a service with high fixed costs and low variable costs. In the case of subway fares, for example, if price discrimination were feasible and permitted the recovery of fixed costs from high-valuing users, it would be efficient for low-valuing users to pay a fare that compensated the state only for the trivial variable costs imposed by their ride.

[22]Even when a user fee recovers actual social costs attributable to a class of users, it may be apportioned among them in a locationally distortive fashion. See, for

12

The provisions commonly called taxes, however, are in their dominant features unlike either user fees or regulation. They tend neither to recover specific governmental costs in the context of a market-style transaction nor to be regulatory so much as revenue-raising devices. Consider, for example, an income tax on salary or a sales tax on consumer purchases. A taxpayer probably does not impose significant costs on society by deciding to work for a salary rather than enjoy leisure or to purchase a consumer item rather than take a walk. Nor is the taxing government likely to be attempting (other than very marginally in its choice of tax base) to discourage work or consumer purchases. The act of earning or purchasing merely serves as a convenient occasion for the government to demand payment.

Taxes emerge from the intersection of two of government's principal characteristics. The first is that it provides public goods, such as police protection, clean streets, and national defense, that cannot be sold separately to individual users through standard market transactions.[23] This limitation prevents governments from charging users directly for many of the benefits provided. The second is that government possesses coercive powers, enabling it to seize property or claim monopolies. Thus, government can successfully extract payments without regard to the cost or value of any benefits provided.

The separation between benefits received and taxes imposed has important implications even if all taxpayers receive an acceptably "fair deal." In particular, it explains why taxpayers should, but are unlikely to, disregard tax costs in making decisions. However much value one receives from the government, one generally does not get

---

example, American Trucking Assos. v. Scheiner, 107 S. Ct. 2829 (1987), holding that fixed highway user charges imposed on truckers unconstitutionally discriminated in favor of in-state truckers who paid the same amount as out-of-staters despite averaging far more miles of use.

[23]Government can also serve the function of redistributing wealth. I do not separately address redistribution here because, to the extent desirable, it can be defined as a public good. If one's goal is a significant transfer of wealth to the poor, for example, one's own efforts may be inadequate if others with money "shirk" their shares of the general transfer. Governmental taxation to redistribute wealth can thus be seen as solving the collective action problem faced by voters with money who favor redistribution. Later I discuss redistribution and conclude that it is most effectively conducted at the national rather than at the state or local level. See chapter 4, the section entitled "Preserving Broad State and Local Autonomy."

more at the margin by increasing one's own tax bill. Thus, tax payments are purely a cost to the taxpayers, and one that bears no direct relationship to either the social cost or the subjective value of the benefits they receive. For society, in contrast, the tax payment itself is a pure transfer (even if its existence and the act of payment have associated costs) that leaves aggregate social monetary wealth unchanged.[24]

In calling taxes revenue raisers devoid of independent regulatory purpose, I have ignored two issues. The first is the problem of classification presented by a tax provision that reflects regulatory rather than revenue-raising purposes. Such a provision can be a revenue-raising tax penalty[25] but perhaps more is commonly a revenue-losing "tax expenditure" that departs from the ordinary course of the tax to serve regulatory purposes, such as homeowners' income tax deductions.[26] Or a provision, while within the ordinary course of the tax, may have been chosen over a comparably plausible alternative for regulatory reasons.[27] In general, for reasons explained in the

---

[24]Tax payments are pure transfers for society even if one believes that all government spending is wasted, so long as the amount and kind of such spending are not affected at the margin by short-term variations in the amount of tax collected. If this spending-invariance condition holds, taxpayers' avoidance of liability merely reallocates the cost of paying for government expenditures, in some hard-to-determine way, from themselves to other current or future members of society. See Daniel Shaviro, "Beyond Public Choice and Public Interest: A Study of the Legislative Process as Illustrated by Tax Legislation in the 1980s," *University of Pennsylvania Law Review* 139 (1990): 1, 59.

[25]Consider, for example, §280E of the Internal Revenue Code, which denies dealers in illegal drugs deductions for certain items that are plainly business expenses, such as rental or salary costs incurred in the illegal business. Such provisions mismeasure income to penalize drug dealing relative to other business activity.

[26]On the tax expenditure concept, see Stanley Surrey, *Pathways to Tax Reform* (Cambridge: Harvard University Press, 1973). The concept rapidly became controversial and has remained so. See, for example, Boris Bittker, "Accounting for Federal 'Tax Subsidies' in the National Budget," *National Tax Journal* 22 (1969): 244; Thomas Griffith, "Theories of Personal Deductions in the Income Tax," *Hastings Law Journal* 40 (1989): 343; Victor Thuronyi, "Tax Expenditures: A Reassessment," *Duke Law Journal* 1988: 1155. While most commonly used in the income tax context, the term *tax expenditure* is equally applicable (or inapplicable) to any other tax that is claimed to have a discernible "normal" structure.

[27]See, for example, William Andrews, "Personal Deductions in an Ideal Income Tax," *Harvard Law Review* 86 (1972): 309, arguing that medical deductions may not be preferential departures from "normal" income tax rules.

section on greater responsiveness of small governmental units in chapter 4, I will emphasize formalism over substance and treat provisions as taxes so long as they are part of the structure of a tax (for example, an income tax deduction or a sales tax exclusion).[28] Second, any basic choice of tax base by a government presumably reflects regulatory purposes regarding how liability ought to be apportioned or the expected behavioral effects of different taxes.[29] These points do not so much rebut the inefficiency of taxes that influence behavior as suggest offsetting benefits or justifications, and I will therefore defer considering them.

We have now seen the grounds for the claim that an efficient tax is one taxpayers ignore. Because this volume examines federalism in taxation, I will focus on locational efficiency to the exclusion of other sorts. Conceptually, a locationally efficient tax is one that does not affect people's decisions about where to live, travel, invest, and so forth. In other words, such a tax replicates as closely as possible the state of affairs that would prevail under a uniform national taxing scheme, disregarding any consequent changes either in the level of taxation or in what is taxed. It may be objected, however, that the case for locational neutrality in taxation is less compelling than the case for other sorts of neutrality—for example, neutrality in the taxation of different types of investment income under an income tax. I will therefore consider the special issues raised by locational neutrality before examining more comprehensively what it means.

The Comparative Value of Locational Neutrality and Tax Neutrality in General

Even if one accepts the view that taxes should usually be neutral and invisible, locational neutrality presents special complexities and difficulties. The key difference between it and, say, neutral treatment of different types of investment income under an income tax is that the cost and value of the services people receive in different geo-

---

[28]See chapter 4, section entitled "Preserving Broad State and Local Government Autonomy."

[29]See, for example, Joseph Isenbergh, "The End of Income Taxation," *Tax Law Review* 45 (1991): 283, arguing that a consumption tax should replace the current income tax to ameliorate the tax system's bias against saving and in favor of current consumption.

graphical areas from their state and local governments are likely to differ, whereas there may be no reason to expect differences in the government services that holders of different types of investments receive.

Consider again my statement that a tax, as distinct from a user fee, involves no relationship between the amount paid and the benefits received. While true at the margin as one's own tax bill increases, it is not necessarily true over a broader range of variation in tax levels. Governments that charge more taxes may often provide more value in the form of services and may be able to direct most of this value to resident taxpayers. These residents, in their capacity as voters, may rationally take a view of taxes different from that in their capacity as taxpayers. Voters are helping to determine everyone's tax burden, not just their own, and therefore have less reason to be tax averse. Voting for higher taxes does not automatically create an externality problem: one may receive significantly more services if everyone pays more. Moreover, even in an individual's capacity as a taxpayer, there may be a relationship between taxes paid and services received. If a government provides insufficient value in exchange for the taxes it extracts, residents may be able to "vote with their feet" by leaving. If exit costs are sufficiently low, state and local taxes *are* user fees, voluntarily exchanged for the state or local government's service package.[30]

In sum, higher taxes in one jurisdiction are not locationally inefficient to the extent that this value is effectively linked to the payment of tax. At least this conclusion is true if one looks at taxpayers only as an undifferentiated class; inefficiency may still result from tax and benefit disparities within the class. Moreover, since voters have some control over taxing levels, we might expect a service offset in cases where voters impose higher taxes on themselves. This point holds even more powerfully if people "vote" in the notional sense of declining to exercise a cheap exit option, since they can decide on their own where to live without needing to be part of a voting majority.

The significance of these points is diminished to the extent that they ignore the tax burden and service benefit disparities within the

---

[30]See, for example, Tiebout, "A Pure Theory of Local Expenditures."

tax-paying class and expect too much both of the often costly exit option[31] and of voting.[32] Thus, at the margin for any one taxpayer, taxes often function simultaneously as costs to the taxpayer and as transfers from society's perspective. Yet the points regarding the benefit and consent of the voter or resident are arguably significant enough to suggest that one particular form of locational disparity merits special attention: the problem of tax exportation, which occurs when governments succeed in placing tax burdens on outsiders.[33] Tax exportation might seem merely a standard case of locational distortion, inducing taxpayers to stay entirely inside the exporting jurisdictions or else avoid them altogether. From the broader perspective, however, tax exportation may pose unusually serious problems by placing tax burdens on what may often be nonconsenting nonbeneficiaries.

So far, in exploring the limits to locational neutrality as a value, I have considered only differences in tax level that result from people's different decisions regarding how much government service to pay for. Differences in tax level may arise, however, even if people in all jurisdictions have identical preferences. The social costs of what all deem to be essential services may vary, because of differences in geography, climate, population density, or any number of other factors. Many of these differences would be efficiently reflected in user fees varying with location if it were feasible to finance all government operations through user fees rather than taxes. How, then, can it be argued that locational neutrality, rather than a system of highly nuanced variation in local tax levels, is optimally efficient?

The answer to this challenge, in part, is that locationally neutral taxation is not optimally efficient. No taxation can be, given that it is an imperfect substitute for user fees, made necessary by the indivisibility of public goods. The argument for locationally neutral taxation,

---

[31]See, for example, Brookes Billman and Noel Cunningham, "Nonbusiness State and Local Taxes: The Case for Deductibility," *Tax Notes* (September 2, 1985), pp. 1107, 1113.

[32]On imperfect information, the danger that one group of voters will exploit another and other standard voting paradoxes and problems, see Iain McLean, *Public Choice* (New York: Basil Blackwell, 1987).

[33]See chapter 4, section entitled "Preserving Broad State and Local Government Autonomy."

17

as for tax neutrality in general, is a *ceteris paribus* argument: that without differences on the service side taxes should be neutral and should minimize the expected behavioral responses to them. The *ceteris paribus* argument is reasonable, however, given the difficulty of measuring the cost or value of government services received by different persons or in different areas, unless the actual variations are quite large.

In other words, despite such actual variations, one should not reject locational neutrality in favor of either a more nuanced standard that incorporates all cost-of-government-service variations or abandonment of the notion of a standard altogether. A nuanced scheme, while theoretically preferable, is too complex and indeterminate to be usable. Moreover, abandoning the locational neutrality standard is unnecessarily skeptical and despairing if it appears plausible that, in most cases, differences in government services received either are not overly significant or will accentuate, rather than offset, the distortive effects of locational disparity in taxation. The leap of faith that support for locational neutrality involves—for such it is, however well founded and sensible—should be familiar to people versed in the income tax policy literature of the past fifty years. For similar reasons, income tax policy is often based on a neutrality norm that ignores both variations in services received by different taxpayers[34] and the arguments for a more nuanced (but too complex and indeterminate) optimal taxation norm, under which rates of taxation would vary with the elasticity of what is being taxed.[35]

Broader Ramifications of Locational Neutrality

Differences between Tax Systems as Inherently Distortive. The previous three sections described the principle of locational neutrality and the reasons for considering it desirable. We saw that it generally requires that taxes not vary with location or affect business or personal decisions regarding location. Although benefits received

---

[34]On the problems with using a benefit standard, see Walter Blum and Harry Kalven, *The Uneasy Case for Progressive Income Taxation* (Chicago: University of Chicago Press, 1953), pp. 451–55.

[35]On optimal taxation, see, for example, Walter Hettich and Stanley Winer, "Blueprints and Pathways: The Shifting Foundations of Tax Reform," *National Tax Journal* 38 (1985): 423, 428.

and voters' or residents' consent may also enter the picture and make taxes the equivalent of user fees that ought to vary with location, those points merely modify rather than eliminate the case for locational neutrality. This section therefore explores the ramifications of locational neutrality in its general sense, leaving the considerations of benefit and consent to be addressed later.[36]

In a locationally neutral system, the level, kinds, and geographical distribution of all activity would be the same as if the country had a uniform national taxing system, disregarding any effects that such a reallocation of taxing authority would have on the types of taxes levied or on tax rates. Unfortunately, this notional touchstone for measuring locational neutrality is not only abstract and counterfactual but also utterly unattainable other than by actually establishing a uniform national taxing system. Consider the administrative and compliance effects of having federal rather than national taxation. The existence of multiple taxing authorities—including, for example, several thousand different sales tax jurisdictions—inevitably creates a burden, unevenly distributed among taxpayers, that changes outcomes. The compliance costs alone of having multiple taxing jurisdictions are great enough, according to one recent commentator, to constitute "a drag on interstate trade almost as debilitating as the border restrictions our federal system was originally designed to prevent."[37]

Even disregarding compliance costs, locational neutrality is unattainable when there are separate taxing jurisdictions as in the United States, unless all jurisdictions enact precisely identical taxes. Assume, for example, that North Dakota has a 10 percent flat-rate income tax on residents and South Dakota has a 5 percent flat-rate income tax on residents. All else being equal, residing in South Dakota is tax favored relative to residing in North Dakota. Or assume that North Dakota taxes real property, while South Dakota taxes sales. Now the locational biases favor owning real property in South Dakota and making sales in North Dakota. Finally, assume that both

---

[36]See chapter 4, section entitled "Preserving Broad State and Local Government Autonomy."

[37]Gordon Henderson, "What We Can Do about What's Wrong with the Tax Law," *Tax Notes* (Dec. 17, 1990): 1349, 1352. See chapter 2, section entitled "The Comparative Value of Locational Neutrality and Tax Neutrality in General," for a discussion of administrative and compliance costs.

states have identical income taxes except that South Dakota allows more favorable depreciation. Even if the states' depreciation rules apply to property owned in other states, the effects are the same as in the rate difference example for taxpayers who own or expect to own depreciable property.

Disparities in tax base present obvious planning opportunities for both taxpayers and governments. The taxpayer side of maximizing aftertax returns by minimizing tax liability is obvious. The government side is significant as well, however. States can choose tax bases that seem likely to draw tax revenues from outsiders. Consider, for example, severance taxes that Alaska, Montana, and Wyoming levy on the extraction of oil or coal (principally for use out of state) or the tendency of states with large tourist industries to charge higher general sales taxes than other states,[38] as well as higher hotel taxes than their general sales taxes.[39] Taxes of this kind penalize interstate relative to intrastate commerce, since wholly in-state items and transactions tend to be more lightly taxed. But any attempt to strike them down involves line-drawing problems if states are assumed to have authority to decide what they want to tax.[40]

Clearly, then, disparities in state and local taxation would defeat locational neutrality even if no person were present in more than one jurisdiction. When taxpayers straddle jurisdictions and thus become directly subject to more than one tax system, the disparities grow worse. The income tax–property tax example above suggested one problem, arising when states have different types of tax bases: the possibility of being either double taxed (as when one has real property in North Dakota and sales in South Dakota) or not taxed at all (if one reverses the states). Yet problems arise even when all states have the

---

[38]John F. Due and John L. Mikesell, *Sales Taxation: State and Local Structure and Administration* (Baltimore: Johns Hopkins University Press, 1983), p. 12.

[39]See, for example, Betsy Wade, "Tax Collectors Lean on the Out-of-Towners," *New York Times*, Aug. 25, 1991, §5, p. 3.

[40]In Commonwealth Edison v. Montana, 453 U.S. 609 (1981), the Supreme Court relied on this assumption to sustain Montana's coal severance tax against constitutional challenge. The Court rejected arguments that the tax unduly exported tax burdens to out-of-staters and exceeded the value of any benefits provided to out-of-staters, largely on the ground that real economic incidence and the value of benefits provided (such as police protection) are prohibitively difficult to measure. I address the merits of the Court's position in chapter 4, section entitled "Preserving Broad State and Local Government Autonomy."

same type of tax base and that base does not in any inherent way target interstate commerce. For each of the major taxes widely employed at the state and local level, a set of coordination problems between jurisdictions, commonly lacking easy solution, has emerged over the years: how to determine which states have taxing authority, and to what degree, over a particular taxpayer or transaction, as well as how one state's exercise of authority should affect another's. Imperfect coordination, while often unavoidable, may distort taxpayers' choices regarding entry into multiple jurisdictions. The following is a brief description of some of the major coordination problems in the principal state and local taxes.

Personal Income Taxes. If income could be taxed only in the state where it was earned and the identity of that state were always clear, the personal income tax might present no coordination problems. At the other extreme, if all states could and did tax all income, regardless of whether the earner or earning activity had any connection with the taxing state, coordination problems would not arise. In that instance, multiple taxation would be a fact of life to which all persons were subject without regard to their locational decisions.

In legal and economic fact, however, neither alternative holds. States can and do tax their residents on all income and nonresidents on income earned within the state.[41] The resulting threat of double taxation when a taxpayer resides in one state and earns income in other states is widely addressed by tax credits for liability incurred elsewhere or by states' declining to exercise their full taxing powers. These countermeasures, however, are not constitutionally required, are not universally employed, and provide incomplete protection because of built-in limitations and disparities in their application.[42]

Double taxation may result even when the states ostensibly try to apportion a person's income, if the location where it was earned (or where one resides) is sufficiently unclear for the states to take inconsistent positions. Yet, even when the states consistently apportion a person's income so that each dollar is taxed only once, his

---

[41]See Guaranty Trust Co. v. Virginia, 305 U.S. 19 (1938); New York ex rel. Cohn v. Graves, 300 U.S. 308 (1937); Walter Hellerstein, "Some Reflections on the State Taxation of a Nonresident's Personal Income," *Michigan Law Review* 72 (1972): 1309, 1310.

[42]See Hellerstein and Hellerstein, *State and Local Taxation*, pp. 968–71.

total tax liability may exceed what it would have been if any one of the states had been the only taxing authority. This consequence results from provisions that limit or prorate personal exemptions, deductions, or credits for persons (such as nonresidents or part-year residents) associated with other states or that count income earned in other states to determine the applicable bracket under a progressive rate structure, meaning that some never benefit from the lower brackets.[43]

A final problem involves the interaction between tax timing and changes in the taxpayer's state of residence. When a state income tax rule permits taxpayers to defer recognizing otherwise taxable income and they move to another state before recognition, then upon recognition both the current and the former state of residence may make a claim, potentially leading to duplicative taxation. This problem has arisen under state income tax rules providing that salary invested in a retirement annuity, along with the annuity fund's inside buildup, is taxable only on withdrawal. States allowing such deferral have attempted to reach withdrawals by taxpayers who move out of state at retirement, leading to overlap with residency-based claims by the taxpayers' new states.[44]

Property Taxes. Not all property taxes present coordination problems. Since real property is generally immobile and has an unambiguous location, its taxation at the state and local level does not ordinarily create coordination problems between different jurisdictions. The main danger to interstate commerce is simply that property assessments are biased against outsiders. Assessment tends to be highly discretionary and is subject to independent administrative review only in four states, plus the District of Columbia.[45]

Mobile personal property presents a danger both of double taxation, if more than one jurisdiction makes a claim, and of tax avoidance, as when taxpayers temporarily move property out of the

---

[43]See Hellerstein and Hellerstein, *State and Local Taxation*, pp. 1346–54; Wheeler v. State of Vermont, 127 Vt. 361, 249 A.2d 887 (1969), appeal dismissed 396 U.S. 4.

[44]See, for example, *Congressional Record* S1159, S1189–1190 (Jan. 24, 1991), describing a bill introduced by Senator Harry Reid to bar states from taxing nonresidents' pension incomes.

[45]See Hellerstein and Hellerstein, *State and Local Taxation*, pp. 192–93.

taxing jurisdiction on tax day.[46] In addition, the taxation of intangible property (such as mortgages or corporate stock) can result in overlapping taxation by different jurisdictions that penalizes taxpayers for multijurisdictional presence. The problem is not only that intangible property may have no clear location but that its value may result from the rights that it conveys in tangible property already subject to property tax. Consider, for example, a property tax on shares of corporate stock held in North Dakota, where all the corporation's tangible property is located and taxed in South Dakota.[47]

Property taxes can yield further coordination problems if the taxpayer's domicile or residency, in addition to the property's location, is a ground for imposing liability. In illustration, Florida's intangible property tax, recently upheld by an evenly divided Supreme Court, applies to items that either have an in-state business situs or are owned by Florida domiciliaries.[48] If other states similarly tax property on the basis of both business situs and domicile, without granting credits for other states' taxes on the same property, multijurisdictional presence is penalized.

Retail Sales and Use Taxes. Perhaps no coordination problem in state and local taxation is better known than that arising under sales taxation. When a buyer in one jurisdiction makes a purchase from a seller in another jurisdiction, both jurisdictions may have a claim. There may be no right answer to where the sale occurred. Moreover, even if the place of sale is clear, residency provides an alternative ground supporting the imposition of a tax. To prevent avoidance of their sales taxes by residents, many jurisdictions impose use taxes on goods purchased out of state but used in state.[49]

As most people who have ordered consumer goods from out of state to avoid sales tax know, however, nontaxation, not double taxation, is the main problem. Pursuant to a Multistate Tax Compact,

---

[46]See ibid., pp. 198–203.

[47]See ibid., pp. 204–7. There is no locational coordination problem (although still double taxation) if North Dakota and South Dakota would have each taxed both the tangible property and the stock if both were located in state.

[48]See Ford Motor Credit Co. v. Florida Dept. of Revenue, U.S. Sup. Ct., No. 88-1847 (May 20, 1991); *Daily Tax Report*, May 21, 1991.

[49]See, for example, Hellerstein and Hellerstein, *State and Local Taxation*, pp. 770–71.

most states accept consistent rules allocating exclusive tax jurisdiction (such as deeming sales to occur in the state of destination) and grant credits where necessary to avoid double taxation.[50] The remaining problems, such as holdouts from this pattern of agreement or the imposition of use taxes that are harsher than the analogous sales taxes and thereby disfavor out-of-state sales, are relatively minor.[51]

A significant coordination problem still remains, but it goes in the opposite direction. While use taxes commonly require self-assessment by the purchaser, collection often depends on the active cooperation of the seller. Given the many thousands of sales tax jurisdictions in this country, however, sellers with nationwide mail or phone order businesses might suffer from intolerable burden if, in keeping with usual sales tax practice, they were required to remit all taxes due from purchasers on their sales to the purchasers' jurisdictions. Although, especially in an age of computers, such a result might not overly burden interstate commerce, the Supreme Court has ruled otherwise. In *National Bellas Hess, Inc. v. Department of Revenue,*[52] the Court held that, at least without congressional authorization, sellers cannot be required to remit the sales tax due from the purchaser to any state where they have not established a sufficient presence to constitute nexus.[53]

The rule of *National Bellas Hess* creates two distortions. First, purchasers often find that they can avoid taxation by making out-of-state purchases, including some that were more expensive before tax than the in-state alternatives. Thus, interstate transactions are tax favored based on the Supreme Court's concern that the only practical alternative is to tax penalize them. Second, sellers are deterred from increasing their presence in a taxing jurisdiction at the margin where it would establish nexus.

A further coordination problem under sales and use taxes arises

---

[50]CCH All States Guide 35, P-H All States Guide ¶701, 29 Vand. L. Rev. 470 et seq. (1976).

[51]See Hellerstein and Hellerstein, *State and Local Taxation,* pp. 781–85. Double taxation of an interstate sale may in any event lead to invalidation of one of the taxes under the commerce clause. See, for example, Goldberg v. Sweet, 488 U.S. 252, 262–64 (1987).

[52]386 U.S. 573 (1967).

[53]The Supreme Court reaffirmed this holding and clarified that Congress could alter the result in North Dakota v. Quill Corp., 112 S. Ct. 1904 (1992).

when states tax sales other than final retail sales. When one state taxes an intermediate sale, for example, of raw materials or services to a manufacturer and another state taxes the final product without allowing a credit for the prior sale, the effect is double taxation of the end product. This problem can of course arise within a single state but may be most likely to occur where states are trying to reach sales that would otherwise escape their jurisdiction—as was suggested recently when Florida abortively imposed a sales tax on services, including many rendered out of state, without limiting the tax to final retail sales.[54]

Business Taxes. States levy a number of taxes on corporations and other business entities. These taxes commonly resemble general income, property, or sales taxes in that they are based on a measure of the taxpayer's profits, value, or gross receipts. Thus, they present many of the same coordination problems as these provisions, but in a particularly significant setting, given that legal entities such as corporations do such a large share of the interstate business in this country.

Taxing companies involved in interstate business would present no coordination problems if each company could be neatly divided, such that each piece belonged for tax purposes to one state. Where the proper lines of division are unclear, however, some pieces may be taxed more than once or not at all, leading to overtaxation or undertaxation of interstate business relative to other business. Historically, the Supreme Court long feared overtaxation more than undertaxation—or else simply interpreted the Constitution's "negative Commerce Clause" with numbing literalness—and therefore barred all direct state and local taxation of interstate commerce.[55]

---

[54]See George Mundstock, "Florida Services: You Only Tax Twice?" *Tax Notes* 35 (June 15, 1987): 1137.

[55]As a literal textual matter, of course, there is no negative commerce clause and thus no possibility of its being interpreted with "numbing literalness." The commerce clause of the Constitution states only that "Congress shall have power . . . To regulate Commerce . . . among the several States," Article I, section 8. This was eventually interpreted as implying what is now called the "negative commerce clause": the proposition that Congress's jurisdiction over interstate commerce is exclusive and that therefore, even in the absence of congressional action, the federal courts can and should strike down improper state and local government infringements of this national power. See, for example, Sholley, "The Negative Implications of the Commerce Clause," pp. 559–83.

The result might be called chronic undertaxation mitigated by judicial myopia, since it allowed indirect taxes on interstate commerce that might be identical to the direct kind in economic incidence and effect.[56] The Court eventually decided, however, that the coordination problem deserved a more sophisticated response. It now holds that interstate business may be taxed, whether directly or indirectly, but that the commerce clause bars undue relative burdens on such commerce, such as duplicative "multiple taxation."[57] The states therefore collectively may reach all the profits, value, or gross receipts of an interstate business but must apportion them among themselves.

The differences between the tax bases of profits, value, and gross receipts, along with the difficulty of defining each, guarantee that states will not achieve the outcome of taxing everything exactly once. States can opportunistically choose whatever base, within the permissible range, appears most favorable to themselves and thereby collectively engage in effective multiple taxation. Businesses can opportunistically exploit disparities in state tax bases in the effort to avoid even single taxation. The Supreme Court, lacking the institutional competence or any plausible ground for picking any one tax base as the right one, may be unable to go beyond crudely weighing the equities case by case or else imposing new formal requirements to replace the old "direct-indirect" line.[58]

Coordination problems would remain even under a uniform tax base, however, because for large interstate businesses there is often

---

[56]See, for example, Hellerstein, "State Taxation of Interstate Business," pp. 42–48; William Lockhart, "A Revolution in Interstate Commerce?" *Minnesota Law Review* (1981): 1025, 1027–34. "Directness" depended, for example, in the case of taxes on commercial freight transportation by interstate railways, on whether the tax was computed with regard to the amount of freight transported (direct and therefore impermissible) or on the proceeds charged by the railway (indirect and therefore permissible). See Hellerstein, "State Taxation of Interstate Business," pp. 43–44.

[57]See, for example, Complete Auto Transit, Inc. v. Brady, 430 U.S. 274 (1977).

[58]An example of a new formal rule to address the multiple taxation problem is the requirement that a tax "have internal consistency—that is, [it] must be such that, if applied by every jurisdiction, there would be no [multiple taxation]." Armco, Inc. v. Hardesty, 467 U.S. 638, 644 (1984). Internal consistency is neither a necessary nor a sufficient condition for multiple taxation, but the Court looks to it because "[a]ny other rule would mean that the constitutionality of [any one state's] tax laws would depend on the shifting complexities of the tax codes of 49 other States." 467 U.S. at 645.

no definite place where gross receipts or income are earned or value exists. The problems go to substance, not just administration or record keeping. Consider, for example, a merger between two previously separate businesses in different states, creating synergies of integration, centralized management, and scale that increase profits and value. Even if everything else remains unchanged, the increased value and income resulting from the synergy do not inherently belong to either state. In any instance where factors of production in more than one state are deployed cooperatively, that which is being taxed may have no "real" location—for example, where income is generated by intangible assets (such as patents) that have no clear location, where contracts are negotiated across state lines, or where property is constructed in one state, transported through a second, and sold in a third.

The difficulty of determining where income, value, or gross receipts are located need not prevent the development of consistent and plausible allocation rules. Such rules may impose social costs of their own as taxpayers plan to minimize tax liability and in some cases enter interstate commerce solely to realize "tax synergies," but at least the rules might solve the basic coordination problem of multiple taxation or nontaxation of a portion of the tax base. While states have in part cooperated and adopted similar rules, complete uniformity has not emerged as a predictable consequence of opportunism and random variation by the states and the courts' lack of institutional competence (or confidence) to impose a uniform rule when no particular rule is clearly correct.

Reflecting the lack of a single correct rule, the federal courts require only that the method of apportionment be reasonable. No tax can be levied without a sufficient nexus, not a very demanding standard that nonetheless deters at the margin establishing an in-state presence.[59] Moreover, at least in principle, extraterritorial value cannot be taxed.[60] Where in-state and out-of-state operations, even if conducted by separate corporations that belong to the same control group, constitute a "unitary business," however—another not very

---

[59]Nexus may be found, for example, if the company maintains an office, employees, or agents to conduct its business, or property in the taxing state. See Hellerstein and Hellerstein, *State and Local Taxation*, p. 362.

[60]See, for example, Container Corp. of Am. v. Franchise Tax Bd., 463 U.S. 159 (1983).

demanding standard that affects incentives at the margin—the state can use any number of apportionment methods in identifying the in-state component subject to tax.[61]

In practice, for income taxation of a unitary multistate business, almost all states employ a three-factor formula based on property, payroll, and sales, but the exact formula and the definition of the three factors vary.[62] While many states weigh all three factors equally, some give extra weight to the sales factor;[63] not surprisingly, these tend to be market states, where the percentage of in-state sales of a national business is likely to exceed the in-state percentage of its property and payroll. Standards other than a three-factor formula are also allowable,[64] even if in practice they clearly favor local residents or businesses, so long as they are not "out of all appropriate proportion to the business being transacted."[65]

Controversy has recently arisen over some states' application of unitary business rules to companies active not just in more than one state in this country but worldwide. A multinational corporate group, if present in such a state, is taxable on the apportionable share of its worldwide income.[66] Taxpayers subject to worldwide unitary taxation have argued against it on a number of grounds, including the following: (1) requiring foreign corporate affiliates to report their taxable income to the United States under U.S. rules creates severe compliance difficulties; (2) since no foreign country engages in worldwide unitary taxation, its implementation here creates effective double taxation of foreign income, along with competitive disadvantage for worldwide businesses relative to those operating purely in state; and (3) the departure of worldwide unitary taxation from

---

[61]In Mobil Oil Corp. v. Commissioner of Taxes, 445 U.S. 425 (1980), for example, Vermont was held entitled to treat Mobil's entire international petroleum operations as a unitary business because a Mobil subsidiary owned and operated a few in-state gas stations.

[62]See Hellerstein and Hellerstein, *State and Local Taxation*, pp. 473–79.

[63]See ibid., pp. 506–8.

[64]See Moorman Mfg. Corp. v. Blair, 437 U.S. 267 (1978).

[65]437 U.S. at 278; see also Joel Michael, "The Constitutionality of Minnesota's Business Tax Credits after Westinghouse Electric Corp.," *Journal of State Taxation* 4 (1985): 163, 167.

[66]See Mobil Oil Corp., 445 U.S. 425.

prevailing domestic practice, both at the national level and in most states, adds to its undesirability.[67] The Supreme Court has held states' use of worldwide unitary taxation constitutionally allowable, however, leaving only a political remedy for those who oppose it.[68]

The basic choice of apportionment formula for unitary businesses, while important, answers only a few of the issues concerning the location of business income that commonly arise. Whenever an activity's location is ambiguous or arguably crosses state lines, how to apply any formula becomes unclear, and a host of competing claims of tax jurisdiction can be made. Consider, for example, a baseball team that plays games in one state during spring training and a number of other states during the season and whose games are broadcast on cable television across the country. Or consider a telephone company that provides interstate calling services, thus arguably entering not only the states in which the parties to phone calls are located but all states through which the phone lines or electrical signals pass. In such situations, states can easily and plausibly take inconsistent positions, under which they may collectively claim more than 100 percent of the income derived from the activities.[69]

In summary, states can choose their apportionment standards opportunistically and make overlapping or inconsistent claims, although such claims will not necessarily lead collectively to overtaxation of interstate business relative to intrastate business. Businesses can also respond opportunistically to coordination problems—for example, by tax planning to minimize liability, deploying superior resources to win contested factual issues at audit, and applying in-state political pressure, backed by the threat of leaving, to obtain favorable rules in the first place.[70]

---

[67]See Charles McLure, *Economic Perspectives on State Taxation of Multijurisdictional Corporations* (Arlington, Va.: Tax Analysts, 1986), pp. 204–8.

[68]See Mobil Oil Corp., 445 U.S. 425; Container Corp. of Am., 463 U.S. 159 (1983).

[69]Other industries that arguably require special apportionment rules include public utilities, railroads, trucks, airlines, insurance companies, and savings and loan associations. See Hellerstein and Hellerstein, *State and Local Taxation*, pp. 498–99.

[70]In one recent case, a corporation was apparently able to exploit differences between states' rules to report only 20 percent of its domestic-source income for

Administrative and Compliance Costs of Disparate State and Local Taxation

While I have thus far emphasized the burdens that state and local taxation deliberately places on interstate commerce, those that arise incidentally may be even more important. The existence of multiple separate tax systems, each with its own set of rules and enforcement personnel, imposes a number of different costs on the national economy. It adds substantially to taxpayers' costs of tax planning and compliance. It increases the costs of tax administration, as each state hires its own bureaucracy and, in many cases, conducts its own audits and imposes its own reporting requirements.[71] It leads to more litigation, in the state courts as well as through federal constitutional challenges. It means that more legislative bodies spend time considering tax law changes and are lobbied by a host of different interests.[72]

The aggregate social costs of all the tax planning, compliance, administration, litigation, and politicking attributable to state and local taxation cannot readily be estimated but are plainly enormous. Although only the avoidable costs are fairly at issue here, state and local tax receipts exceed $400 billion annually; for sales taxes (which are the best documented), rough estimates suggest that the costs of state government tax administration plus direct costs of taxpayer compliance equal almost 5 percent of the amount collected.[73] Even

---

federal tax purposes as income of any state. See "Little Support Seen for Proposals to Harmonize State Taxation of Intangibles," *Daily Tax Report*, October 10, 1991.

[71]See Jeffrey A. Dubin, Michael J. Graetz, and Louis J. Wilde, "United States" in *Administrative and Compliance Costs of Taxation* (International Fiscal Assn. ed., 1989), pp. 329–36.

[72]Of course, high lobbying costs are desirable to the extent that they deter lobbying that one considers undesirable. One disadvantage to the tax base coordination that I ultimately recommend is that it may increase the return to interest groups, by lowering the cost of changing all jurisdictions' rules and increasing the return to changing the rules set at the national level.

[73]Due and Mikesell, *Sales Taxation*, pp. 323–25, estimate state administrative costs at 0.73 percent and taxpayer compliance costs at 3.93 percent of the revenue collected through sales taxation—totalling 4.66 percent. A more recent study by the State of Washington estimates administrative costs at 0.93 percent. State of Washington Dept. of Revenue, Program Admin. Section, *Tax Administration Survey* 20 (1988) [hereinafter *Washington Tax Survey*].

in the unlikely event that the sales tax's impressive level of collection efficiency holds across the board,[74] annual administration and compliance costs for all state and local taxes would approach $20 billion annually.[75]

Unnecessarily high compliance costs are an inevitable consequence of state and local government autonomy in defining tax bases even under optimistic assumptions about interstate cooperation. Even assuming that everyone generally wants to cooperate, the positive transactions costs of cooperation, along with the occasional countervailing factors motivating legislators, suggest that at least residual differences will remain between states' tax bases, as suggested by the substantial but incomplete degree of state "piggybacking" onto the federal definition of taxable income. Even a small residual degree of variation may impose substantial compliance costs, however—for example, by requiring duplicative record keeping regarding tax attributes such as loss carryovers and basis. Compliance costs are not purely proportional to the quantum of divergence between states' tax bases; a significant fixed cost results from the bare fact of divergence.

In particular, divergence requires taxpayers: (1) to know about a host of different rules; (2) to exercise judgment about the application of different jurisdictions' rules; (3) to engage in separate numerical calculations (often the least of the problems in a computer age); (4) to keep duplicative records, for example, of an asset's basis under different income tax regimes; (5) to file multiple forms—not only tax

---

[74]The sales tax may be above average in collection efficiency. In particular, compared with state income taxes, it concentrates compliance costs on a relatively small number of persons—the retailers who are responsible for collecting it—thus potentially creating scale efficiencies, and it is unlikely to elicit anything near the same level of tax planning. Moreover, while for many taxpayers the state income tax presents relatively light marginal burdens due to federal income tax "piggybacking," for multistate businesses—admittedly, a small group that substantially overlaps with retailers—the extra costs of state and local taxation are increased by income allocation issues. Finally, Washington's tax administration survey estimates state collection costs for the sales tax as lower than those for business or income taxes. *Washington Tax Survey*, p. 20.

[75]This number, however, is unrealistically low because it excludes such costs as tax planning, litigation, and politicking. While political activity may be viewed as valuable in itself, rather than as a social cost, that view seems relatively inapplicable to the straightforward economic lobbying by interest groups that undoubtedly accounts for a large portion of the political activity in the tax area.

31

returns, but information reports, requests for extensions, reports of tax return adjustments required by other jurisdictions, and the like; and (6) to engage in a host of parallel interactions with government officials, such as auditors and legislators.

These burdens, while not entirely avoidable given the existence of multiple governmental units, need not be nearly so great as they are in practice. The following is a brief description of the features of each of the principal state and local taxes that create arguably unnecessary burdens.

Personal and Business Income Taxes. Despite substantial piggy-backing by state and local governments onto the federal income tax base, enough differences remain, along with legal or factual issues and compliance requirements unique to the states and localities, to create substantial added compliance costs. Several companies that I contacted during my research indicated that they devote as much manpower and other resources to state and local income taxation as to federal income taxation. This effort suggests that, at least for multistate businesses, compliance efficiency (compliance costs in relation to taxes paid) is lower for state and local income taxes than for federal income taxes, even treating all shared compliance requirements as attributable to the federal taxes. While a company's state and local income tax bills may occasionally exceed its federal income tax bill—for example, if it has net taxable income in several states but not for its total operations—federal income tax liability is ordinarily higher, given the higher federal marginal rates and aggregate federal tax revenue.

The compliance burdens faced by multistate businesses—and at times by individuals—arise at several different conceptual stages. First comes the problem of identifying the taxpaying unit. In particular, consolidated corporate groups must determine the set of affiliates subject to tax in each state. Not only may the set of affiliates with direct jurisdictional nexus vary from state to state, but also the legal standards may vary for determining both nexus and which members of the groups are engaged in a unitary business, obviating the need for direct nexus by each separate affiliate. Even if the legal issues are clear, tax record keeping by the group may be complicated by the varying sets of in-state taxpayers. Moreover, if some affiliates are deemed outside the state's taxing jurisdiction, transactions between the inside and the outside affiliates may be reviewable under state provisions analogous to Internal Revenue Code section 482, which empowers the IRS commissioner to reallocate income among affiliated taxpayers across national boundaries.[76] Section 482 is a notorious quagmire that involves factual complexity and lacks a clear underlying standard. The commissioner often seeks to reconstruct the true arm's-length terms of an intercorporate transaction, but such terms often do not exist and would depend in large part on the outcome of bargaining that never occurred. States nonetheless have begun to take an interest in issues similar to those arising under section 482.[77]

The possible application of worldwide unitary taxation creates additional costs for multinational companies. Where such taxes are applicable, taxpayers must procure information from foreign affiliates that may be reluctant to provide it and that may not keep records similar to those required for federal income tax purposes. Even some states that follow, or permit as an election, a "water's-edge rule," under which foreign affiliates are excluded from the tax-paying group, require taxpayers to file comprehensive spreadsheets detailing their income and operations on a worldwide basis.[78] These spreadsheets are generally not required annually, but the length of time between required filings varies from state to state.[79]

An additional issue in identifying the tax-paying unit arises for small, closely held companies. For federal income tax purposes, such a company may elect to be classified as an S corporation, the income of which is taxed directly to its shareholders rather than being taxed itself, under rules resembling those for partnerships.[80] Eight states, however, decline to recognize S corporation status for their own income tax purposes.[81]

---

[76]See, for example, California Revenue and Taxation Code Section 17551.

[77]I learned while interviewing companies' tax staffs that Connecticut has been raising Section 482 issues and that California recently sent tax personnel to Section 482 training sessions.

[78]Taxpayer elections tend to be socially undesirable even if politically popular, in that they encourage taxpayers to substitute compliance costs that are dead-weight social costs for tax payments that are transfers.

[79]This information was derived from my interviews with companies' tax staffs.

[80]See I.R.C. §§1361.

[81]See Commerce Clearing House State Tax Guide, ¶10–0 (1990).

Once the precise tax-paying unit is known, taxpayers must determine the potential tax base within each state's reach. States follow different income apportionment formulas—in some cases, for example, giving extra weight to the sales factor in a variety of degrees.[82] Even where the formulas are ostensibly the same, their precise meaning may differ. As an example, the includability, and if includable the location, of intangible property and income under what appear to be identical formulas may raise questions. Other potential tax-base issues that create burdens include determining what municipal bond interest is tax exempt (since most states, unlike the federal government, exempt only the interest on their own municipal bonds) and identifying for deduction disallowance the expenses attributable to income that a given state does not tax.[83]

A third stage in income tax compliance involves applying the rules for determining taxable income once the potential tax base is known. States' rules for computing taxable income vary from the federal rules and from each other in a number of different respects. California and New York, for example, have their own depreciation systems for business property. All property subject to these systems therefore has a different basis, and potentially a different amount of gain or loss upon taxable transfer, from that for federal tax purposes.[84] Other states, while generally following the federal depreciation rules, require that a portion of federal depreciation deductions be added back to taxable income. Five states reject federal depletion rules, and five others have modified them in varying degrees.[85] Net operating losses and capital loss carryovers are allowed everywhere, but with a range of different carryover periods. Foreign income taxes are, variously, creditable (with an election to deduct them instead) as under the federal income tax, deductible only, or disregarded

---

[82]See Hellerstein and Hellerstein, *State and Local Taxation*, pp. 506–8. For example, New York double-weights the sales factor for regular tax (although not minimum tax) purposes; Illinois, Connecticut, Kentucky, Massachusetts, and Ohio simply double-weight the sales factor; and Minnesota's three-factor formula is weighted 70-15-15 in favor of sales.

[83]I.R.C. §265 is a federal example of such a rule.

[84]An item of property may also have different bases for state and federal income tax purposes owing to differences in the allowance of tax credits that give rise to basis adjustments.

[85]See *Commerce Clearing House State Tax Guide*, ¶10–060.

34

altogether (the predominant state rule for corporate taxpayers). States may tax foreign or out-of-state dividends received by a corporation under a variety of different rules. States provide different investment incentives like, for example, rewarding investment in designated enterprise zones. Eight states levy an alternative minimum tax, payable to the extent that it exceeds the amount due under the regular tax, to reduce the value of tax preferences.[86]

A fourth stage in income tax compliance is reporting to state tax commissions. The tax return is only one of many documents that must be filed separately for each jurisdiction on its own forms. In addition, thirty-one states require separate applications for an extension of time to file the tax return, instead of granting extensions automatically when granted by the federal government.[87] States typically require that all adjustments to federal income tax returns be reported to them, but both the form and the deadline for making such reports differ.

A fifth and final stage in income tax compliance is the audit process. States generally conduct their own audits of major corporate taxpayers. These audits typically take from several days to several weeks, tend to be influenced more by political and budgetary considerations than federal income tax audits are, often take the form of nonspecific denials that particular deductions or other tax benefits are allowable (requiring voluminous documentation in response), and are conducted very much in light of the taxpayer's expected unwillingness to litigate unless large amounts or broadly important principles are at issue.[88]

Property Taxes. The compliance costs resulting from property taxes differ in kind from those resulting from income taxes in two respects. First, property taxation is predominantly used by local governments, while income taxation is predominantly used by state governments.[89]

---

[86]See ibid., ¶10–104. The alternative minimum tax, in comparison with the regular tax, is computed by applying a lower rate to a larger base (because of the denial of specified tax preferences). Pennsylvania, while not levying an alternative minimum tax, treats certain tax preferences as modification addbacks to taxable income.

[87]See *Commerce Clearing House State Tax Guide*, ¶10–115. This counts both states that do not honor the federal extension and those that honor it upon application.

[88]This information was derived from my interviews with companies' tax staffs.

[89]See, for example, Hellerstein and Hellerstein, *State and Local Taxation*, pp. 7,

Second, the difficult or unclear issues that need to be resolved in determining one's liability for property taxation are to a greater extent factual rather than legal.

The first of these differences makes property tax compliance more of a "retail" in contrast with a "wholesale" operation than state and local income tax compliance. More separate jurisdictions, and more individual officials compared with the amount of revenue at stake, are involved. With decision making so localized, the computation of property tax liability can be more subjective, political, and dependent on the intervention of persons (such as local attorneys) with working relationships with tax administrators.

The greater emphasis of property tax compliance on factual rather than on legal issues further adds to the subjectivity of property tax assessment. The difference from income taxation is relative, though, not absolute. Income taxes frequently pose case-specific issues of fact, such as what was the section 482 arm's-length transfer price for an item transferred by one corporate affiliate to another, or which of a company's expenses related to tax-exempt income. Property tax liability often turns on questions of law, such as what categories of property are taxed at what rates and exactly how these categories are defined. Jurisdictions not only recognize different categories of property for rate purposes—for example, real property, personal property, equipment, inventory, intangible property, and the like—but define what is ostensibly the same category in a variety of ways.

Nonetheless, for property taxes, case-specific factual issues have relative prominence because of the centrality of valuation. The amount of property tax due typically depends on the property's value, rather than, say, on its historical cost. Although some jurisdictions apply formulas to known data, determining a property's value frequently requires the exercise of judgment, often culminating in an administrator's subjective assessment of conflicting expert testimony.

The differences in kind between the compliance costs of income taxes and property taxes do not make one tax better or worse than the

---

10, stating that in the mid-1980s, state governments derived 37.6 percent of their revenue from income taxes and 1.9 percent from property taxes, whereas local governments derived 37.7 percent of their revenue from property taxes and 3 percent from income taxes.

other. The differences are relevant chiefly to questions such as which tax's compliance costs could more easily be reduced and which tax involves a greater risk of discriminatory application in administration. The differences suggest that, barring significant changes, compliance costs are more easily reduced and discrimination against interstate commerce more easily eliminated for state and local income taxation than for property taxation.

Retail Sales and Use Taxes. From a compliance standpoint, retail sales and use taxes resemble income taxes in one sense and property taxes in another. Like income taxes, they often turn simply on the numbers, such as the gross revenues derived from sales transactions, rather than routinely requiring the exercise of judgment about indefinite facts. As with property tax compliance, however, tax compliance for retail sales and use is itself a "retail" rather than a "wholesale" operation for multistate businesses. This country has about 7,000 separate sales tax jurisdictions.[90] Often, even neighboring jurisdictions within the same state impose different classifications and rates, collect their own taxes separately, impose separate documentation requirements (such as the use of their own certificates attesting to tax exemption or that taxes have been paid), and conduct their own audits. Incentives for local jurisdictions to cut their costs by either cooperating or delegating administrative duties to state governments may be outweighed at times by the political desire to impose diverse rules (with the effect of impeding cooperation or delegation) or by the interest of local bureaucracies in maintaining their power and function.

The compliance costs incurred by sellers pursuant to their legal obligation to remit sales taxes due from purchasers are significantly increased by the need to comply with so many separate jurisdictions. The burden results not only from parallel or duplicative paperwork but also from the requirement to know and understand each jurisdiction's rules. As with property taxes, not only the rates but also the categories (and precise meanings of these categories) to which rates

---

[90]See Advisory Committee on Intergovernmental Relations, *Significant Features of Fiscal Federalism*, vol. 1 (1989), pp. 58–59, table 1; *ABA Sales and Use Tax Handbook*, D. Michael Young and John T. Piper, eds. (1988). When National Bellas Hess was decided, the number of such jurisdictions was about 2,300. National Bellas Hess, 386 U.S. 573, 759 n.12 (1967).

and exemptions apply often vary between jurisdictions. Moreover, burden arises from the need under provisions of state use taxes that, pursuant to *National Bellas Hess*, require determining nexus for a large number of separate jurisdictions, and before that to engage in tax planning regarding nexus.

Other Taxes. State and local governments impose a vast array of other taxes, along with licenses, user fees, and other charges that may serve in part to raise general revenue and thus be conceptually indistinct from taxes. A recent growth area is environmental taxes, which may often serve both environmental and revenue-raising objectives. The sheer number and variety of such charges (whether or not "taxes" under my definition) can create massive compliance costs for nationwide businesses, particularly if there is substantial intrastate variation or if laws change rapidly.

In some cases, the structure of these taxes suggests a lack of concern by state and local governments about taxpayers' compliance costs. One example is severance and excise taxes on mineral extraction, which often take the form either of a "netback" based on mineral value (so called because it requires "netting back" from the contract price to the value of the mineral deposit by subtracting production costs) or of a "volumetric" tax based only on the quantity extracted. Netback taxes impose significantly greater burden than volumetric taxes, not only because of the additional records and computations that they require but also because of the fact-specific judgmental issue of what costs are appropriately subtracted from the contract price. Netback taxes nonetheless continue to be widely used.[91]

Responding to the Problems Caused by Locational Disparity

This section has suggested the magnitude and intractability of the locational disparities resulting from federalism in taxation. Merely having different tax rates or bases defeats locational neutrality and is

---

[91]The principal advantage of the netback method (since rates can be adjusted to yield the same revenue under either method) is that it automatically, without requiring the legislature to amend the rates, adjusts for changes in the value of the minerals, which might be thought somehow to correlate with the appropriate (or revenue-maximizing) level of tax.

thus economically similar to having tariffs imposed at state borders. Differences between state and local tax systems also give rise to serious coordination problems, potentially inducing taxpayers to seek or avoid a multijurisdictional presence purely for tax reasons and presenting strategic opportunities, as for tax exportation or protectionism, to state and local governments. Such differences also impose massive costs of compliance, administration, tax planning, politicking, and litigation.

One might take some satisfaction from the fact that taxpayers and state and local governments both have strategic opportunities, since perhaps a rough balance would emerge between the taxation of interstate and intrastate activity, except for two sobering considerations. First, the opposing forces do not offset in all cases; instead, there are "pockets" where one side has the decisive advantage, resulting in significant overtaxation or undertaxation. As an example, Alaska's and Wyoming's capacity to tax natural resources consumed mainly by outsiders gives them a special opportunity to engage in significant tax exportation—or at least to persuade themselves that they are doing so, although the actual economic incidence of their severance taxes may be unclear.[92] This perception of spending other people's money may not only encourage the two states to burden interstate commerce—an effect of their taxes regardless of incidence—but also remove the political discipline that ordinarily constrains waste in government spending. Alaska and Wyoming lead the country in per capita government expenditure—with Alaska spending five times, and Wyoming two times, the national average, and anecdotal evidence indicates that they waste much of the excess, rather than spending it productively.[93] Even if they spent the excess relatively productively, the difference in spending might be undesirable if based on the special opportunity to tax resources consumed by outsiders, rather than on a voter preference for more government services.

Second, even if the tax burdens on intrastate and interstate

---

[92]See, for example, McLure, "Tax Exporting and the Commerce Clause," pp. 29–35.

[93]See, for example, Dwight R. Lee, "A Bigger Oil Spill That No Alaskan Seems to Notice," *Wall Street Journal*, September 20, 1989. An alternative explanation for Alaska's and Wyoming's high per capita spending is that their low population densities deny them economies of scale in providing government services.

activity are roughly equivalent in general, the result may still be allocatively inefficient. Opposing inefficiencies of overtaxation and undertaxation of interstate commerce in different sectors of the economy may compound each other as distortions, rather than cancel each other out. Moreover, shifts between interstate and intrastate commerce are only one category of allocative inefficiency resulting from federalism in taxation. Other examples include the shifting of investment to low-tax jurisdictions, to activities whose proper apportionment between jurisdictions is unclear and manipulable, and to more mobile forms of capital, which can flee when jurisdictions raise their taxes.[94]

Costly departures from locational neutrality are inevitable under a federal system. If we accept the framers' starting point of wanting both a federal system and some sort of antitariff principle that constrains departures from locational neutrality (without being limited to what are tariffs on their face), we encounter an intellectual quandary. How are we to define and identify impermissible departures from locational neutrality, given that many departures will be permitted? Particularly if courts are in charge of applying the antitariff principle, some sort of general legal standard is needed; courts presumably cannot be quite so ad hoc as legislatures in weighing each case on its individual merits.

The legal standard most widely accepted in this area is one barring discrimination against outsiders or interstate commerce. The leading Supreme Court authority concerning state taxation of interstate business, *Complete Auto Transit v. Brady*,[95] lists four requirements for upholding such taxes, the most stringent and important of which is the absence of discrimination against interstate commerce.[96] Among commentators, the antidiscrimination standard stands out even more clearly as a dominant, if not quite exclusive, legal norm.[97]

---

[94]See Fred McChesney, "Rent Extraction and Rent Creation in the Economic Theory of Regulation," *Journal of Legal Studies* 16 (1987): 101, 108.

[95]430 U.S. 274 (1977).

[96]The other three factors are the existence of a nexus with the taxing state, fair apportionment where there is interstate activity, and a fair relationship to the services provided by the taxing state. 430 U.S. at 279, 287. On the greater stringency and importance of the antidiscrimination requirement, see Hellerstein, "State Taxation of Interstate Business," pp. 60–62; Tatarowicz and Mims-Velarde, "An Analytical Approach to State Tax Discrimination," p. 884.

[97]See, for example, Paul J. Hartman, *Federal Limitations on State and Local*

What constitutes discrimination against outsiders or interstate commerce is far from clear.[98] Yet a bedrock illustration is both simple and intuitive. For North Dakota to impose a 10 percent income tax, while South Dakota imposes a 5 percent income tax would create locational distortion but not discrimination, since North Dakota's tax applies alike to all taxpayers, both in state and out of state. By contrast, for North Dakota to tax out-of-state businesses at 10 percent and local businesses at 5 percent would be discriminatory.[99] The following chapter explores more thoroughly both the meaning of a federal judicial standard barring discrimination against outsiders or interstate commerce and whether this standard provides a workable and attractive fallback from requiring complete locational neutrality.

Taxation (Rochester, N.Y.: Lawyers Cooperative Publishing Co., 1981); Laurence Tribe, *American Constitutional Law* ¶ 6–17 2nd ed. (Mineola, N.Y.: Foundation Press, 1988); James F. Blumstein, "Some Intersections of the Negative Commerce Clause and the New Federalism: The Case of Discriminatory State Income Tax Treatment of Out-of-State Tax-Exempt Bonds," *Vanderbilt Law Review* 31 (1978): 473, 497–518; Walter Hellerstein, "State Taxation and the Supreme Court: Toward a More Unified Approach to Constitutional Adjudication?" *Michigan Law Review* 75 (1977): 1426, 1446; Lockhart, "A Revolution in Interstate Commerce?" pp. 1034–38; Regan, "The Supreme Court and State Protectionism," pp. 1115–18, articulating an "antiprotectionism" standard that resembles barring discrimination; Michael E. Smith, "State Discriminations against Interstate Commerce, *California Law Review* 74 (1986): 1203, 1213; Tatarowicz and Mims-Velarde, "An Analytical Approach to State Tax Discrimination"; Mark V. Tushnet, "Rethinking the Dormant Commerce Clause," *Wisconsin Law Review* 1979: 125, 130–31.

[98]See, for example, Ernest J. Brown, "The Open Economy: Justice Frankfurter and the Position of the Judiciary," *Yale Law Journal* 67 (1957): 219, 228; Hartman, *Federal Limitations on State and Local Taxation*, pp. 2–19; Hellerstein, "State Taxation of Interstate Business," p. 60.

[99]See, for example, West Point Wholesale Grocery Co. v. Opelika, 354 U.S. 390 (1957), striking down a tax that applied solely to merchants outside the taxing jurisdiction.

3
The Exercise of Federal Judicial Review to Bar Discrimination against Outsiders or Interstate Commerce

WHILE THE NOTION of discrimination against outsiders or interstate commerce seems easy to grasp intuitively, it has proved slippery
in practice. Some dismiss it as a "shibboleth,"[1] while even the more
hopeful concede that it is "not self-defining" and can appear "delu-
sively simple."[2] Essentially, discrimination is a specific form of
locational nonneutrality, founded on comparing two groups—the
persons inside and the persons outside the taxing jurisdiction or,
alternatively, the commerce originating inside and the commerce
originating outside. Since the groups being compared are taken as
given, the antidiscrimination standard reflects an assumption either
that taxes have no effect at the margin on where one resides or locates
one's business or that any such effect is irrelevant. After all, low
taxes as an inducement to move in (such as South Dakota's 5 percent
rate in the earlier example) are permissible, and a claim of discrimination cannot be rebutted by arguing that if only victims moved into
the taxing jurisdiction, they would no longer be discriminated
against. Instead, outsiders are compared with insiders as they stand
and are deemed victims of discrimination if, in cases where members
of the two groups are alike in some relevant sense, the tax system

---

[1]Brown, "The Open Economy," p. 228.

[2]Hartman, *Federal Limitations on State and Local Taxation*, ¶2:19, p. 116; Tatarowicz and Mims-Velarde, "An Analytical Approach to State Tax Discrimination,"
p. 885.

treats the outsiders worse, either by directly taxing them more or by otherwise imposing a burden that places them at a competitive disadvantage.[3]

Below, I examine why the antidiscrimination standard is often thought appealing—specifically, why discrimination may be considered worse than other types of locational disparity, what it should be construed to mean, and how workable a standard it provides. I then turn to the problems in defining and applying the standard.

Why Bar Discrimination While Permitting Other Locational Disparity?

The antidiscrimination standard is highly selective in addressing locational distortion. In addition to placing taxpayers in two fixed groups, insiders and outsiders, and ignoring marginal effects on which group one chooses to join, it treats one of the two groups, the outsiders, as needing unique protection. It does not bar discrimination against insiders, for example, to attract outside investment. Moreover, given the requirement of nexus (that outsiders potentially subject to tax must have entered the taxing jurisdiction at least to a limited extent), the antidiscrimination standard reflects an assumption that marginal effects on such limited entry are important, in contrast with marginal effects on where one primarily resides or locates one's business.

The reasons for the antidiscrimination standard's selective focus are easily deduced. Presumably, the focus on marginal effects on limited entry into a jurisdiction, while ignoring such effects on primary residence or business location, reflects a judgment that the marginal effects on limited entry are more elastic, and thus more

---

[3]See, for example, Goldberg v. Sweet, 488 U.S. 252, 265–66 (1987), stating that the commerce clause requires neither facially discriminating against outsiders nor apportioning a larger share of the tax burden to interstate commerce; Hartman, *Federal Limitations on State and Local Taxation*, p. 127: "commercial advantage to local business at the expense of out-of-state business"; Hellerstein, "Constitutional Limitations on State Tax Exportation," p. 22: "greater burdens on out-of-state goods or activities than on competing in-state goods or activities"; Regan, "The Supreme Court and State Protectionism," p. 1126: "improve the competitive position of local economic actors, just because they are local, vis-à-vis their foreign competitors"; Smith, "State Discrimination against Interstate Commerce," p. 1213: "greater burdens on those outside the state, to the advantage of those within."

substantially disrupted by disparate taxation, or else more likely in practice to draw state and local governmental hostility (since once one fully joins a community one may have a greater chance of being treated as well as the other members). The decision to intervene only when outsiders are disadvantaged, not when they are advantaged, reflects the judgment that insiders' exclusive political representation as voters leaves the outsiders uniquely vulnerable.[4]

As Mark Tushnet has noted, however, this political explanation for the antidiscrimination standard, while superficially appealing, misses an important point.[5] Outside merchants (or consumers) ordinarily have grounds for hoping that in-state political processes will reflect their interests, even aside from the possibility that their campaign contributions will be accepted like any other. When they are taxed discriminatorily, they rarely suffer alone. Their actual or prospective in-state customers (or merchants) typically suffer with them, bearing some portion of the tax burden or losing the opportunity to buy (or sell) desired goods. Indeed, it is plausible that, in most cases where a state discriminates against interstate commerce, it reduces its own well-being on balance.[6] Discriminatory taxes are thus not purely products of a lack of political representation after all. Rather, they result from the interaction of that problem with a well-known public choice problem of intrajurisdictional politics: that widely dispersed groups with low individual stakes (such as consumers) suffer from collective action and information cost problems relative to concentrated groups with high individual stakes (such as producers in particular industries).[7]

The argument for barring discrimination against outsiders or interstate commerce therefore has less to do with political represen-

---

[4]See, for example, South Carolina Highway Dept. v. Barnwell Bros., 303 U.S. 177, 184 n.2 (1938); and Tribe, *American Constitutional Law*, pp. 408–13.

[5]Tushnet, "Rethinking the Dormant Commerce Clause," pp. 132–33. Tribe makes the same point as Tushnet but dismisses it without further analysis for the sin of "turning traditional Commerce Clause analysis on its head," *American Constitutional Law*, p. 413.

[6]In the paradigmatic case of tariffs on both imports and exports, this has been well known at least since Adam Smith. See Adam Smith, *The Wealth of Nations*.

[7]See Mancur Olson, *The Logic of Collective Action* (Cambridge, Mass.: Harvard University Press, 1971); and Tushnet, "Rethinking the Dormant Commerce Clause," p. 133.

tation than one might have thought. Accordingly, one might question the antidiscrimination standard for using federal judicial powers to address intrastate distributional issues or, alternatively, for reaching only a part of what Mancur Olson called the "systematic tendency for 'exploitation' of the great [in number] by the small."[8] Or one might want to complicate the standard by applying it with an eye to just how deficient in-state political processes seemed in the particular case.[9] One might, for example, be more tolerant of questionable statutes in cases where, at the time of enactment, the issue of effects on consumers was widely discussed, in-state consumer groups were well organized, or some of the adversely affected narrow interest groups were from in state.

While the Supreme Court has occasionally articulated the political representation argument for barring discrimination against outsiders or interstate commerce,[10] it has only sporadically examined whether significant in-state political forces were on the losing side.[11] The Court may not understand the underlying public choice problem well enough to consider in any consistent fashion the significance of adversely affected but politically unorganized in-staters. This lack of understanding would explain the recent case of *Goldberg v. Sweet*,[12] where the Court stated that a tax paid by in-state consumers on their out-of-state telephone calls was constitutionally innocuous because the consumers could complain as political insiders and "it is not a purpose of the Commerce Clause to protect state residents from their own state taxes."[13] To follow this principle consistently—which the

---

[8]Olson, *The Logic of Collective Action*, p. 29.

[9]Tushnet seems to suggest this; see "Rethinking the Dormant Commerce Clause," p. 133.

[10]See, for example, Southern Pacific Co. v. Arizona, 325 U.S. 761, 767–68 n.2 (1945); South Carolina Highway Dept. v. Barnwell Bros., 303 U.S. 177, 184 n.2 (1938); and Cooley v. Board of Port Wardens, 53 U.S. (12 How.) 299, 315 (1851). See also Tribe, *American Constitutional Law*, p. 410.

[11]But see South Carolina Highway Dept. v. Barnwell Bros., 303 U.S. at 187, upholding a questionable statute that directly affected in-staters in large numbers; Raymond Motor Transp., Inc. v. Rice, 434 U.S. 429 (1978), invalidating a statute that barred large tractor-trailers from state highways but provided exemptions that applied to many in-staters); and Kassel v. Consolidated Freightways Corp., 450 U.S. 662 (1981) (same).

[12]488 U.S. 252 (1989).

[13]488 U.S. at 266.

45

Court has not done[14]—would either eliminate most negative commerce clause scrutiny by making adverse impact on in-staters a defense (probably beyond the Court's intention) or else revive the old formalist distinction between "direct" and "indirect" taxes, with the issue now being whether local consumers (rather than interstate commerce as previously) were taxed directly or only indirectly.[15]

Other than a relative lack of political representation, the antidiscrimination principle could rest on one of three alternative bases. Each base shares with the representational view a potential to influence how one would want to define discrimination. First, the "enmity between states" ground for objecting to tariffs, which I rejected earlier as less important than locational neutrality, could be revived here now that we are considering distinctions within the category of nonneutral taxes.[16] This ground would presumably suggest striking down state and local taxes that visibly and obviously harmed outsiders, while paying less heed to taxes with uncertain or well-disguised effects.

Second, one could object morally or aesthetically to states' subjective intentions to harm outsiders, on the ground that such intentions are—in the words of Donald Regan—"inconsistent with the very idea of a political union."[17] Under this view, it need not matter whether a particular tax has actual distortionary effects or is perceived by outsiders as hostile, although one might expect strong positive correlation on both points. This ground suggests focusing on a subjectively defined discriminatory intent and striking down statutes that on analysis exhibit such intent even if the harm to outsiders or interstate commerce is uncertain or well disguised.

Finally, one could object equally to all locational distortion but single out discriminatory taxes for opportunistic reasons. Such taxes

---

[14]As Justices Stevens and O'Connor noted in concurrences, numerous Supreme Court precedents have recognized that interstate commerce is impermissibly burdened when in-staters are penalized for engaging in it. 488 U.S. at 268, 270. In Boston Stock Exch. v. State Tax Commn., 429 U.S. 318 (1977), for example, the Court invalidated a securities transfer tax on state residents that discriminated against out-of-state sales.

[15]The Court in Goldberg purported to rely on the economic burden of the challenged tax, which it assumed was the same as the direct incidence. 488 U.S. at 266.

[16]See chapter 2, section entitled "The Harms to Be Avoided."

[17]Regan, "The Supreme Court and State Protectionism," p. 1113.

may be the easiest to oppose politically since the term *discrimination* is so pejorative or the Constitution may afford grounds for judicial intervention in these but not in other cases.[18] Opportunism's only apparent implication for the meaning of discrimination is that it be made as broad as possible.

For better or worse, we have largely been spared overt reliance by the Supreme Court on any of these grounds for distinguishing discrimination against outsiders or interstate commerce from other locational distortion. The perception standard perhaps could not be openly followed in any case, as it appears unprincipled and may be difficult to apply. Any suggestion that it secretly motivates the Court was contradicted by *Commonwealth Edison v. Montana*,[19] upholding a state's transparent and politically controversial attempt to shift tax burdens to outsiders by simultaneously reducing various in-state taxes and increasing a coal severance tax that, at least in the short run, out-of-state consumers principally paid.[20] The discriminatory intent standard is conceded by its principal scholarly advocate not to explain state and local tax cases,[21] and its lack of influence is suggested by *Commonwealth Edison* and other recent cases where the state's intention was fairly clear.[22] Opportunism, in the sense of striking down taxes that create locational disparity whenever a case

---

[18]I ignore the nonopportunistic argument that we should simply do what the Constitution says for its own sake, because I am here discussing policy, not constitutional interpretation. As discussed in chapter 3, section entitled "Attempts to Make the Discrimination Standard Coherent," however, it is far from clear that the framers intended or expected courts to discern and vigorously enforce a "negative commerce clause."

[19]453 U.S. 609 (1981).

[20]On the political controversiality of Montana's severance tax, see, for example, Hellerstein, "Constitutional Limitations on State Tax Exportation," p. 75.

[21]See Regan, "The Supreme Court and State Protectionism," p. 1186.

[22]See, for example, Moorman Mfg. Corp. v. Blair, 437 U.S. 267 (1978). Moorman upheld Iowa's use of a single-factor test (based only on sales) for apportioning the interstate income of a unitary business. The test, in contrast with the three-factor test used by forty-four other states (based on property, payroll, and sales), obviously benefited Iowa, predominantly a market state, sufficiently to suggest to a recent commentator that "it takes no great feat of imagination to conjure up the legislative purpose underlying the Iowa statute." Walter Hellerstein, "Commerce Clause Restraints on State Taxation: Purposeful Economic Protectionism and Beyond," *Michigan Law Review* 85 (1987): 758, 765.

for "discrimination" can be made, even more plainly has not guided the Supreme Court's lurching course, which instead has been tempered by what Laurence Tribe calls "an extra dose of judicial sympathy for state taxing power."[23]

In sum, the Supreme Court has largely ignored the relevant but potentially highly complicating question of whether the reasons for focusing on discrimination against outsiders or interstate commerce should shape the definition of discrimination. Nonetheless, as we will see below, the antidiscrimination standard has an almost excruciating vagueness and inconsistency in practice, partly because of the Court's mistakes and erratic behavior in interpreting it but more fundamentally because of the standard's built-in difficulties.

Theoretical and Historical Difficulties in Defining Discrimination

The question now arises whether, given antidiscrimination's limited focus, it is reconcilable with state and local taxing power, as locational neutrality is not. The answer, unfortunately, is no. Only one type of locational neutrality problem is eliminated by narrowing one's gaze as antidiscrimination dictates: that resulting when jurisdiction impose different tax rates (as when North Dakota taxes all instate income at 10 percent, and South Dakota at 5 percent, but each state's rate applies to insiders and outsiders alike). Problems resulting from the use of different tax bases remain. The very existence of inconsistent tax bases creates the possibility that outsiders alone will in effect be taxed more than once (or not at all), and states may opportunistically choose tax bases designed to shift tax burdens to outsiders or interstate commerce. Yet it may seem plausible to regard

---

[23]Tribe, *American Constitutional Law*, p. 442. Consistent leaning either in favor of or against state taxing power is particularly unlikely given the lack of clear ideological guideposts. A harsh line against state and local governments' exercise of their taxing powers is judicial activism protecting persons against the government on the one hand and support for business against government on the other. Perhaps reflecting this lack of clear guideposts, the conservative Justice Scalia consistently takes the governments' side, while the conservative Richard Epstein generally takes the taxpayer's side. See Richard Epstein, "Taxation, Regulation, and Confiscation," *Osgoode Hall Law Journal* 20 (1982): 433, 445–59. The liberal Justice Marshall took the business taxpayer's side in *Commonwealth Edison* and the government's side in *Moorman*.

the power to choose one's own tax base as central to the sovereignty of state and local governments.

Coordination problems further impede identifying instances of discrimination. The lack of clear answers to how to allocate even consistently defined tax bases among the states creates the possibility that a given allocation method may lead to relative overtaxation of interstate commerce, whether resulting from states' opportunism or simply from their making different decisions.

Short of imposing uniform tax bases and coordination rules, we cannot expect state and local taxation never to harm any outsiders relative to any insiders. Concern for state and local autonomy may seem to require allowing some flexibility and perhaps even some disparate impact on outsiders, so long as it remains within reason. Moreover, we may not want to err too much on the side of protecting outsiders, given their strategic opportunities to minimize their tax burdens and the reasons for wanting to tax them neutrally, not preferentially.

Consequently, an antidiscrimination standard, like a broader locational neutrality standard, is fundamentally in tension with state and local government autonomy. Once autonomy is given counter-vailing weight, the standard's capacity to yield consistent and pre-dictable decisions evaporates. One must weigh the facts case by case, even if guided by general principles such as that discriminatory intent mandates application of a stricter rule of invalidity.[24] Realism must flourish, if at all, at the expense of predictability, and judges' idiosyncratic responses to particular sets of facts become prominent.

At the same time, formalism is hard to banish altogether. Realistic considerations too complicated for a court to consider systematically—such as whether a particular tax rate is too high,[25] whether an interstate business is overtaxed given all fifty states' constantly changing laws (and if so which states' laws should change),[26] and whether the apparent discrimination in one part of a state's tax code is cured by some offsetting feature elsewhere in the code[27]—may be thought necessary to ignore even if their import is

---

[24]See Bacchus Imports, Ltd. v. Dias, 468 U.S. 263, 270 (1984).

[25]See Commonwealth Edison Co., 453 U.S. 609, 628 (1981).

[26]See Armco, Inc. v. Hardesty, 467 U.S. 638, 644–45 (1984).

[27]See American Trucking Assos. v. Scheiner, 107 S. Ct. 2829, 288–89 (1987).

clear in a particular case. Moreover, if one believes (as many do) as a premise of American federalism that states must have the right to set their own tax bases, one way of achieving discriminatory effect—indirectly, through a tax base designed primarily to reach outsiders but that does not on its face treat them differently—inevitably does better than other methods from which it may differ only in form.[28] Thus, the antidiscrimination standard can lead to the worst of both worlds: all the unpredictability of attempted realism and all the arbitrariness and circumventability of formalism.[29]

This unfortunate potential has been all too richly realized in practice. Even the Supreme Court, while bravely forging ahead, repeatedly confesses that its decisions form a "quagmire"[30] that "leaves much room for controversy and confusion and little in the way of precise guides to the States in the exercise of their indispensable power of taxation."[31] This harsh judgment has become enough of a truism that it need not be proven anew here.[32] Nonetheless, to show the magnitude of the problem and its relationship to the antidiscrimination standard's underlying confusion, it is worth briefly exploring the Court's repeated tendency in this area to contradict itself or

---

[28]See Commonwealth Edison Co., 453 U.S. at 624–25; and Moorman Mfg. Corp. v. Blair, 437 U.S. 267, 280 (1978).

[29]See Complete Auto Transit v. Brady, 430 U.S. 274 (1977), disparaging the earlier constitutional era's formal rule distinguishing direct from indirect burdens for "stand[ing] only as a trap to the unwary draftsman."

[30]See, for example, Northwestern States Portland Cement Co. v. Minnesota, 358 U.S. 450, 457 (1959); and Boston Stock Exchange, 429 U.S. 329; Scheiner, 107 S. Ct. at 280.

[31]Northwestern States, 358 U.S. at 457; Boston Stock Exchange, 429 U.S. at 329; see also Scheiner, 107 S. Ct. at 269: "The uneven course of decisions in this field reflects the difficulties of reconciling unrestricted access to the national market with each State's authority to collect its fair share of revenues from interstate commercial activities."

[32]See, for example, Hartman, *Federal Limitations on State and Local Taxation*, pp. 52–54; Hellerstein, "State Taxation of Interstate Business," p. 81; Tribe, *American Constitutional Law*, p. 439; see also Gunther, *Constitutional Law*, pp. 332–33 (11th ed. 1985), declining even to discuss, in an otherwise comprehensive constitutional law treatise, the constitutional issues raised by state and local taxation because the "intricacies . . . would require more time and space than the undertaking warrants"; Julian N. Eule, "Laying the Dormant Commerce Clause to Rest," *Yale Law Journal* 91 (1982): 425, 426 n.2, declining to synthesize dormant commerce clause tax cases because they are so confusing and complex.

decline to follow a consistent approach, even when it is not, as happens frequently, consciously overruling a precedent[33] or announcing a new test.[34] The following sample of inconsistencies and odd juxtapositions in recent cases concerning state taxes should help bring to light the difficulties, both inherent and self-inflicted, with which the Supreme Court has been struggling.

• Are courts institutionally capable of examining the rate or level of a state tax to decide whether it is reasonable? *Commonwealth Edison* says no in the context of a coal severance tax,[35] while *American Trucking Assos. v. Scheiner* says yes in the context of a flat tax on truckers' use of in-state highways.[36]

• *Commonwealth Edison* and *Scheiner* are similarly at odds on the question of how to determine whether a tax imposed on outsiders is justified by the benefits they derive from the state government.[37] According to *Commonwealth Edison,* the question requires no detailed factual inquiry but is automatically satisfied where the state exercises its police powers and thus provides the "benefits which it has conferred by the fact of being an orderly, civilized society" to all who pass through.[38] The case rejects the taxpayer's argument that only costs and services directly related to coal extraction were relevant to the comparison of tax and benefit. In *Scheiner,* however,

---

[33]See, for example, Complete Auto Transit v. Brady, 430 U.S. 274 (1977), overruling Spector Motor Service v. O'Connor, 340 U.S. 602 (1951); Armco, Inc. v. Hardesty, 467 U.S. 638, 642 (1984), endorsing the dissent in General Motors Corp. v. Washington, 377 U.S. 436 (1964); Scheiner, 107 S. Ct. at 299 (O'Connor, J., dissenting, noting that the Court directly overrules the holdings of three cases directly on point that it had cited with approval only nine years previously, and after issuing Brady to overrule Spector).

[34]See, for example, Complete Auto Transit, 430 U.S. (four-part test for taxes on interstate business); Container Corp. of America v. Franchise Tax Bd., 463 U.S. 159, 169–70 (1983), announcing new "internal consistency" and "external consistency" tests for the allocation of multijurisdictional business income.

[35]Commonwealth Edison v. Montana, 453 U.S. 609, 628 (1981).

[36]Scheiner, 107 S. Ct. at 289–90, deeming tax "excessive" and distinguishing from reasonable flat fees that were significantly lower.

[37]Complete Auto Transit v. Brady, 430 U.S. 274 (1977), describes this as a requirement apart from discrimination for upholding a tax on interstate commerce, but notionally it appears related, since charging the same tax for fewer services is arguably a kind of discrimination.

[38]Commonwealth Edison, 453 U.S. at 624–28.

the tax had to "approximate fairly the cost or value of the use of Pennsylvania's roads."[39]

• Anticipating *Scheiner's* can-do approach to problems of measurement, the Court in *Moorman Manufacturing Corp. v. Blair* is willing to draw lines between extreme and moderate disparities in the tax burdens imposed on interstate business.[40] *Moorman*, therefore, permits the use of a single-factor income allocation formula that overattributes income from interstate commerce to the taxing jurisdiction, thus creating relative burden, so long as the disparity is not too great.[41] *Moorman* distinguishes *Hans Rees' Sons, Inc. v. North Carolina ex rel. Maxwell*,[42] in which a state's single-factor allocation formula was struck down, because there the disparity between the scope of interstate operations and the in-state allocation of income was greater.[43] Apparently, then, line drawing is not a problem (unlike in *Commonwealth Edison*), and some burden on interstate commerce is allowable but not too much. In *Bacchus Imports, Ltd. v. Dias*,[44] however, we learn, in the context of a tax exemption for local business, that no discrimination against interstate commerce is allowable.[45] The state cannot argue that the burden is only slight. In short, where it is difficult to measure burden precisely, the answer may be to allow no burden (as in *Bacchus*), some burden (as in *Moorman*), or any and all burden (as in *Commonwealth Edison*).

• Perhaps *Bacchus* is special because it concerned a tax that, by exempting local businesses, on its face discriminated against interstate commerce.[46] The meaning of such discrimination is by no means clear, however. In *Tyler Pipe Industries v. Washington State Department of Revenue*,[47] a tax was described as "facially discriminatory" where it required both local and outside manufacturers to

---

[39]Scheiner, 107 S. Ct. at 290.

[40]437 U.S. 267 (1978).

[41]437 U.S. at 274.

[42]283 U.S. 123 (1931).

[43]Moorman, 437 U.S. at 274.

[44]468 U.S. 263 (1984).

[45]468 U.S. at 269, citing Maryland v. Louisiana, 451 U.S. 725, 760 (1981).

[46]468 U.S. at 268–71.

[47]483 U.S. 232 (1987).

pay a wholesale tax on sales in state and locals alone to pay a manufacturers' tax in lieu of the wholesale tax (but calculated at the same rate) on their sales out of state.[48] In short, "facial discrimination" was found even though the statute explicitly treated in-staters and outsiders alike except where it taxed only the in-staters.[49] By contrast, in *Boston Stock Exchange v. State Tax Commission*,[50] the Court apparently regarded as neutral a state tax that, analogous to the Washington wholesale tax, applied exclusively to sales in state, here of securities that were transferred or delivered in state by either in-state or outside stock exchanges.[51]

• The problem in *Tyler* was that other states might charge a wholesale tax on Washington exports or a manufacturer's tax on Washington imports, thus leading to double taxation of interstate commerce. (This danger was equally presented by the statute the Court called "neutral" in *Boston Stock Exchange*.) Yet in *Moorman*, where Iowa used an allocation almost certain to create multiple taxation of interstate commerce, there was no discrimination on the face of the formula. The only apparent difference is that in *Moorman* the threat of multiple taxation was deducible only if one knew certain clear and undisputed facts about other states' income allocation rules and Iowa's status as a market rather than a producer state, whereas in *Tyler* the threat was abstractly deducible if one assumes knowledge of basic Supreme Court nexus doctrine.[52] Accordingly, whether a tax is discriminatory on its face when it creates a danger of multiple taxation depends not just on the face of the statute but on what types of facts (among the broader set available to the relevant state actors) need to be known to demonstrate a significant danger. This distinction apparently is so important that in *Moorman* the Court dismissed a strong showing of actual multiple taxation as overly "speculative,"[53] whereas in *Tyler* it stated that actual multiple taxation need not be

---

[48]483 U.S. at 244.

[49]483 U.S. at 256–57 (Scalia, J., dissenting).

[50]429 U.S. 318 (1977).

[51]See 429 U.S. at 330, approving *in dicta* of a tax that was the precursor to the one being litigated. Justice Scalia noted the contradiction in his Tyler dissent. 483 U.S. at 255 (Scalia, J., dissenting).

[52]See Hellerstein, "Commerce Clause Restraints on State Taxation," p. 132.

[53]Moorman, 437 U.S. at 280.

shown for the statute to be invalidated.

• The Court desires, to the extent possible, to rely on the "practical consequences" and "actual effect" of state taxation, not on "metaphysic[s]" or "legal terminology."[54] Yet cases such as *Tyler*, by applying an "internal consistency" test to strike down state taxes that would burden interstate commerce if enacted by more than one jurisdiction, create a peculiar formal distinction, given the states' basic discretion to decide what they want to tax. Whereas the hypothetical double taxation that would arise if two states enacted similar taxes is constitutionally intolerable, the actual double taxation that results from existing dissimilar taxes is permissible.[55] If, for example, state A taxes in-state manufacturing only and state B taxes in-state sales only, taxpayers may have no constitutional complaint, even though companies exporting from A to B face multiple taxation and even though the states may be able to predict what tax bases will tend to favor in-state businesses or taxpayers.[56]

• As far as the Supreme Court has openly said, internal consistency remains a substantive requirement in the state and local tax area. Yet in a recent case, *Ford Motor Credit Co. v. Florida Department of Revenue*, an evenly divided Court (with Justice O'Connor not participating) upheld without opinion a tax that plainly violated the requirement.[57] The tax at issue in this case applied to intangible property that either had an in-state situs or was owned by a Florida domiciliary. Its unambiguous effect, therefore, if adopted by all jurisdictions, would be to double-tax all intangible property that was located in one state and owned by a domiciliary of another state.

• According to *Bacchus* and *Westinghouse Electric Corp. v. Tully*,[58] striking down a New York state investment tax credit that applied only to in-state investment, states may not "foreclose tax-neutral investment decisions . . . in an attempt to induce business operations to be performed in the home State that could more efficiently be performed elsewhere."[59] Yet other decisions explain that states may

---

[54]Scheiner, 107 S. Ct. at 294–95.

[55]See Tyler, 483 U.S. at 258–59 (Scalia, J., dissenting).

[56]See Armco, Inc. v. Hardesty, 467 U.S. 638, 645 (1984).

[57]U.S. Sup. Ct. No. 88-1847, May 20, 1991.

[58]466 U.S. 388 (1984).

[59]Westinghouse, 466 U.S. at 406, quoting Boston Stock Exchange v. State Tax Commn., 429 U.S. 318 (1977).

"structur[e] their tax systems to encourage the growth and development of intrastate commerce and industry" and to "compete with other States for a share of interstate commerce."[60] *Westinghouse* regards as particularly significant that the credit, since computed by determining the New York state percentage of the taxpayer's total investment, "not only . . . 'provide[s] a positive incentive for increased business activity in New York State,' . . . but also penalizes increases in . . . activities in other States."[61] *Bacchus*, by contrast, rejects the distinction between a "benefit" and a "burden," and between the motives of helping in-state producers and harming outsiders.[62]

• Despite the ostensible lack of distinction between benefits and burdens, states may in some situations discriminate in favor of local businesses relative to outsiders if the mechanism is a direct spending program rather than the tax system. The only definite limitation on favoring in-state businesses through direct subsidies is that the state act as a "market participant," or buyer of goods, rather than as a regulator.[63] The underlying notion is that states, as sovereign entities, must be permitted to buy the goods of their choice and, if they so prefer, to deal solely with their own citizens.[64] Yet this rule has been held to apply even when the state is not in any real sense using the goods it purchases—for example, when it pays private parties to destroy inoperable cars.[65] Moreover, there apparently is no bar on overpaying local sellers or bidding up the market price to their advantage.[66]

• As noted earlier, *Goldberg v. Sweet* denies that the commerce

---

[60]Armco, 467 U.S. at 645–46.

[61]466 U.S. at 400–01.

[62]468 U.S. at 273.

[63]See Reeves, Inc. v. Stake, 447 U.S. 429 (1980); White v. Massachusetts, U.S. (1983); Michael, "The Constitutionality of Minnesota's Business Tax Credits," pp. 184–87; Hughes v. Alexandria Scrap, 426 U.S. 794 (1976). In addition, states may not be allowed to favor local businesses through overly pervasive and open-ended discriminatory spending programs. See Michael, "The Constitutionality of Minnesota's Business Tax Credits," p. 187.

[64]See Reeves, 447 U.S. at 441.

[65]See Hughes v. Alexandria Scrap, 426 U.S. 794, (1976).

[66]See Hughes, 426 U.S. at 806.

clause protects in-state residents against discriminatory taxation. Numerous earlier cases, however, explicitly hold to the contrary where in-staters were subjected to a higher tax rate on interstate than on intrastate transactions.[67]

As the above instances show, legal doctrine in the state and local tax area is shot through with uneasy juxtapositions and outright contradictions. Some of the disparities may be explainable in a principled and convincing fashion. The internal consistency test, for example, may eliminate a category of taxes burdening interstate commerce that courts can easily identify and states cannot easily replace with other discriminatory taxes. Other disparities may be isolated mistakes, such as the dictum from *Goldberg v. Sweet*,[68] or unannounced changes in legal standard, such as *Ford Motor Credit*.[69] Yet the Supreme Court's lurching course clearly reflects underlying conceptual problems. Surely its performance, from a technical and consistency standpoint, is not always this bad.[70]

In part, the Supreme Court's error has been to look for the middle, implicitly balancing aversion to discrimination against concern for state and local autonomy. Strangely, the Court apparently regards the tax area as justifying *greater* deference to state and local government autonomy than commerce clause cases involving regulation.[71] This preference seems exactly backwards. To the extent that state and local taxes serve only revenue-raising, not regulatory, purposes, the taxing government may have little stake in their particular form, and they should be relatively substitutable. Thus, compare the severance tax upheld in *Commonwealth Edison v. Montana* to a famous example of regulation with interstate effects: a

---

[67]See, for example, Tyler, 483 U.S. 232 (1987); Westinghouse, 466 U.S. 388 (1984).

[68]488 U.S. 252 (1987).

[69]Ford Motor Credit Co. v. Florida Dept. of Revenue, U.S. Sup. Ct., No. 88-1847 (May 20, 1991).

[70]Negative commerce clause jurisprudence has long been an area of relative weakness for the Court. See, for example, David Currie, *The Constitution in the Supreme Court: The First Hundred Years 1789–1888* (Chicago: University of Chicago Press, 1985), p. 234.

[71]See Tribe, *American Constitutional Law*, p. 442; Kitch, "Regulation and the American Common Market," p. 31.

Wisconsin city's rule, struck down in *Dean Milk Co. v. City of Madison*, that milk had to be pasteurized within five miles of the city center, ostensibly to facilitate plant inspection by city officials.[72] While Montana's need for revenue could plainly have been met by other taxes, the lack of need for the *Dean Milk* rule at issue cannot be assumed until one examines the facts. *Dean Milk* was an easy case solely because the sham nature of the city's health concerns and the underlying protectionist motive were so transparent. If the health justifications had been plausible, however, the case would have been difficult, given the importance of allowing Madison to protect its residents against unsafe milk and the presumably limited ways of doing this conveniently.

The Supreme Court may treat tax cases as meriting greater deference to state and local governments than regulation cases because it regards the power to tax as the heart of a government's sovereignty. Another explanation is that the Court simply lacks confidence in its ability to understand tax cases and resolve them intelligently, thus preferring to let most challenged taxes stand.[73] While both explanations may be persuasive descriptively, neither provides much support for the normative proposition that the Supreme Court should defer. Effective sovereignty, while requiring an ability to raise revenue, depends less strongly on the power to choose a particular means of revenue raising. Indeed, the relative substitutability of one revenue-raising device for another suggests that state and local government sovereignty may be less threatened by judicial review of taxation than of regulation. As for the Court's lack of understanding of tax cases, a better course than relaxing judicial review of these cases would be to achieve greater competence in deciding them. In the final chapter of this book I suggest legal standards that should make adequate performance by the courts more feasible.[74]

Some might argue that, even if the Supreme Court's heightened deference to state and local taxation is not always justified, in today's political and economic environment it makes sense. Over the past

---

[72]340 U.S. 349 (1951).

[73]These explanations were suggested to me by Richard Briffault and Henry Monaghan, respectively.

[74]See chapter 5, section entitled "The Federal Courts."

few years, state and local governments have borne an increasing share of the responsibility for providing government services, and this, along with obligations for transfer payments, has strained their fiscal capacity. Increased need for revenue, however, cannot justify greater judicial deference when it principally derives from voters' unwillingness—reflected as well in national budget deficits—to pay through taxes for the services that they wish their governments to provide. If anything, the current fiscal situation at the state and local level, by creating greater incentives for tax exportation, calls for more careful judicial scrutiny.[75]

Thus, the Supreme Court should reverse its current practice and defer *less* to state and local government autonomy in tax cases than in regulatory cases. Despite the inherent problems with the discrimination concept, this approach would enable the Court to perform in the area far more coherently and predictably. Alternatively, if the Court viewed the discrimination standard as overly vague even with this improvement, it might move in the opposite direction and replace its current balancing with a general refusal to strike down state and local tax provisions. Both directions of doctrinal movement have their advocates, and below I consider prominent examples of both.

Attempts to Make the Discrimination Standard Coherent

The previous argument showed that an antidiscrimination standard is inherently flawed. Yet improvement may conceivably be possible, especially if the countervailing notion of state and local autonomy is given either far less or far more weight, pushing balancing problems to the margin. Thus, two recent proposals are worth examining. The first is Ferdinand Schoettle's proposal that ideas from public finance economics, and in particular comparison of the marginal tax costs of

---

[75]Surely every state in this country has sufficient wealth within its borders to finance government services and transfer payments at less than confiscatory rates. To the extent that states cannot raise additional revenue because increased taxation would prompt exit, the answer (where the affected government spending is desirable) is to shift financing to the national level. There might, in some instances, be a second-best argument for tax exportation as correcting the misallocation of properly national spending functions to the state and local level, but it seems plausible that the dominant marginal effect of tax exportation will generally be to increase spending for the benefit of state and local residents, which should generally be financed by them rather than nationally.

in-state and outside businesses, be employed more openly and consistently.[76] The second is Justice Antonin Scalia's view that the courts should bar only discrimination that appears clearly on the face of the taxing statute.[77] I will explore these proposals in turn.

The Comparative Marginal Cost Standard. Schoettle argues that the Supreme Court has done far worse than necessary in its treatment of state and local taxation, largely because of its taste for simple catch phrases at the expense of case-specific economic analysis. He urges the Court to replace its ever-changing bevy of tests with detailed factual examination of the single question: "Does the challenged tax have effects that place interstate commerce at a disadvantage?"[78] He insists this question can be addressed intelligently by persons who lack formal economic training, so long as they keep in mind a basic principle of price theory: that firms decide whether to sell at a given price by comparing that price to the marginal cost of a sale, not to any measure or fraction of their total coasts. He deduces from this principle that marginal, not total, tax costs need to be equalized between in-state and outside businesses and that courts should therefore require such equality from state and local taxes.[79]

Two of Schoettle's illustrations help explain his point. First, a source rule for income taxation, under which states can tax only the income earned in-state, preserves equality of marginal cost between residents and nonresidents who are considering limited entry. If the state could tax the outside income of an outsider who earned any income in state, that outsider's tax cost of initial entry would exceed an insider's tax cost of increasing his in-state business by the same amount (since his preexisting in-state business would already be subject to the state's income tax).[80] Schoettle admits that income often has no clear geographical source, and he does not address,

---

[76]See Ferdinand Schoettle, "Facts, Law, and Economics in Commerce Clause Challenges to State Taxes," *Tax Notes* 50 (March 11, 1991), p. 1149.

[77]See especially Scalia's dissent in Tyler, 483 U.S. 232 (1987).

[78]Schoettle, "Facts, Law, and Economics," p. 1150.

[79]Ibid., p. 1151.

[80]Ibid., pp. 1153–54. Similar problems presumably arise when one's state of residence taxes income earned in other jurisdictions, since then, without tax credits or other adjustments, one pays the other state's income tax (if any) plus one's own.

presumably as beyond the scope of a plausible constitutional analysis, the point that all differences between state or local taxes distort market decisions even under a perfectly applied source rule.[81]

Second, Schoettle argues that double taxation of interstate commerce is not distortive where taxpayers face equal marginal costs. He posits a case akin to my example where North Dakota had a property tax and South Dakota a sales tax. While a company is double-taxed if it uses property in North Dakota to make widgets for sale in South Dakota, its entry into South Dakota is not thereby competitively handicapped. Since the property tax is a preexisting fixed cost, only the sales tax is a marginal cost of entry, and therefore the North Dakota business can compete with South Dakota businesses for sales in South Dakota without competitive disadvantage.[82]

This example might be criticized as insufficiently dynamic in its assessment of the effects of state and local taxes. What if a North Dakota firm considers building an improvement to its in-state property, thus increasing its North Dakota tax bill, to produce additional widgets for sale in South Dakota? Now the added North Dakota property tax *is* a marginal cost. More generally, one might expect firms that were deciding where to locate widget plants to choose South Dakota, all else being equal, thereby disadvantaging business in North Dakota at the margin.[83]

Or consider *Tyler Pipe Industries,* where the Supreme Court struck down Washington's application of a wholesale tax on in-state sales, whether by local or foreign firms, and a manufacturing tax on goods exported by local firms. The Supreme Court struck down the tax under the internal consistency test that Schoettle criticizes as overly ad hoc.[84] His test would seem to have several different

---

[81]Ibid., p. 1153.

[82]Ibid., p. 1154. Schoettle follows this example with one where, if a state had both a property tax and a sales tax but gave a tax credit for the former against the latter to avoid double taxation of its own businesses, it would thereby discriminate against interstate commerce, since in-state businesses, even if paying about the same total tax as outsiders, would have lower marginal costs of making additional sales.

[83]To be sure, the differences in the two states' taxes would also favor interstate commerce, by encouraging companies to locate in South Dakota and sell in North Dakota, but Schoettle correctly notes that advantaging interstate commerce is as inefficient as disadvantaging it. Ibid., pp. 1151–52.

[84]See ibid., p. 1150.

plausible applications here, however. If the manufacturing tax is treated as a given, in-state firms are tax favored at the margin since they avoid it by manufacturing for the home market. If the manufacturing test is regarded as wholly separate, however, then within the Washington market all firms are taxed alike. Yet if other states also have manufacturing taxes, then at the margin the outside firms are taxed more heavily. But this consequence is the result of the combination of two jurisdictions' decisions—the very point made by application of the internal consistency test—and it is unclear to what extent, if any, each jurisdiction should have to give way.

To be administratively workable, Schoettle's test might require a relatively narrow view of what tax costs are marginal in particular cases. This limitation would reduce its power to address locational distortion without completely eliminating the line-drawing issues of deciding whether a particular tax cost is marginal or fixed. Three further conceptual and line-drawing issues are also worth noting. First, given the difficulty of tracing the sources of income from a multistate business, what should be done about a case like *Moorman*, where Iowa used an aggressively self-serving rule on sources, in the absence of a "correct" rule? Given the fortuity that almost every other state used some variant of a single, more sophisticated rule, the case may be easy for Schoettle: Iowa loses. If the dominant sourcing rule grew less clear over time, however, one would encounter line-drawing problems in deciding when only Congress could prescribe a uniform rule. Moreover, should Iowa lose under Schoettle's standard after all? He has no objection to double taxation per se, and any imperfect sourcing rule will have the distortive effects that he describes. Such distortions include a mismatch between the actual increase in income that results from one's entering a new jurisdiction and the amount of income attributed to that jurisdiction and the tax planning motivated by the sourcing rule itself, for example, inefficiently keeping employees out of a high-tax state that uses payroll in its allocation formula.

Second, Schoettle's standard does not address tax exportation. The coal severance tax in *Commonwealth Edison v. Montana*, for example, does not disadvantage interstate commerce if one compares in-state with outside users of coal (who are taxed alike). It is disadvantageous only if one compares coal to products that are not exported to nearly the same extent. This is a standard problem for questions of discrimination throughout the law: what is the appropriate comparison?[85] Assuming that the severance tax is discriminatory because of the obvious singling out of an item that is predominantly exported, one again has a line-drawing problem regarding less clear-cut cases.

Third, Schoettle treats the receipt of benefits from state spending as irrelevant to the tax issue.[86] While for most purposes I make the same assumption, it is worth recalling that tax payments and benefits received may correlate to some extent.[87] In *Commonwealth Edison*, for example, even aside from the marginal costs imposed on Montana by coal mining, which should presumably be recovered through a levy (whether termed a tax or a user fee), what about the Supreme Court's suggestion that almost any level of tax was appropriate given the benefits flowing to outsiders from Montana's exercise of police powers to maintain a basic level of civilization? This analysis may have been extremely weak[88]—indeed, the Court seems to have feared as much, self-consciously denying that the reference to maintaining civilization was "a disingenuous incantation"[89]—but was not inherently implausible. Maintaining civilization is a public good, and public goods may be undersupplied by voters if only they, not nonvoting beneficiaries, are taxed to pay for such goods. Thus, one might think it efficient to require outsiders to make some contribution toward Montana's exercise of police powers.

These various problems reflect less on Schoettle's ingenious contribution to commerce clause thinking than on the basic intractability of the underlying issues. Very likely his standard, applied with a more consistent judicial solicitude for interstate commerce in cases (such as *Moorman* and *Commonwealth Edison*) where the standard's implications are unclear, would significantly improve the law, making it more coherent, predictable, and better focused on a real set of

---

[85]Compare Louis Eisenstein, *The Ideologies of Taxation* (New York: Ronald Press Co., 1961); David Strauss, "Discriminatory Intent and the Taming of Brown," *University of Chicago Law Review* 56 (1989): 935, 940–46.

[86]Schoettle, "Facts, Law, and Economics," p. 1160.

[87]But see chapter 2, section entitled "The Comparative Value of Locational Neutrality and Tax Neutrality in General," where I discuss the problems with ignoring the benefit side.

[88]See, for example, Epstein, "Taxation, Regulation, and Confiscation," p. 445.

[89]Commonwealth Edison v. Montana, 453 U.S. 609, 628 (1981).

economic distortions than the prevailing "quagmire."[90] Yet the inherent problems with an antidiscrimination standard that his proposal cannot eliminate should be kept in mind as we ask whether we want courts to be active in the first place in the state and local tax area. This is the very question that underlies Justice Scalia's position.

Justice Scalia's Standard. Justice Scalia, in a series of recent concurring and dissenting opinions in state tax cases, denounces what he views as systematic judicial overreaching.[91] Rather than "expanding our beachhead in this impoverished territory," Scalia suggests at most "being satisfied with what we have already acquired by a sort of intellectual adverse possession."[92] To this end, although on a clean slate he might virtually eliminate federal judicial review of state and local taxes,[93] he advocates barring only the discrimination that occurs when a provision on its own terms taxes outsiders more heavily than insiders.[94]

Justice Scalia relies principally on the lack of textual support for the negative commerce clause, since the text mentions only Congress's positive power to regulate interstate commerce, and on his belief that no such provision was intended by the framers.[95] Yet he also finds reasons of policy for his position, arguing that the Court has produced a "quagmire" that "makes no sense" for reasons rooted

---

[90]Thus, I recommend, in chapter 5, section entitled "Constitutional Limitations on Congressional Power," that Schoettle's standard be used as one part of the Supreme Court's negative commerce clause analysis.

[91]See Tyler Pipe Indus. v. Washington State Dept. of Revenue, 483 U.S. 232, 254 (1987); American Trucking Assos. v. Scheiner, 107 S. Ct. 282, 303 (1987); Goldberg v. Sweet, 488 U.S. 252, 271 (1987); American Trucking Assos. v. Smith, 110 S. Ct. 2323, 2343 (1990).

[92]Scheiner, 483 U.S. at 265 (Scalia, J., dissenting).

[93]Justice Scalia would still bar "rank" state tax discrimination against outsiders under the privilege and immunities clause of the Constitution. Scheiner, 107 S. Ct. at 265 (Scalia, J., dissenting). Whether this differs from facial discrimination is unclear.

[94]Tyler, 483 U.S. at 257–59 (Scalia, J., dissenting). Justice Scalia would confine his inquiry to the contested provision itself, not to the state's entire tax code. Scheiner, 107 S. Ct. at 305 (Scalia, J., dissenting).

[95]Tyler, 483 U.S. at 260–64 (Scalia, J., dissenting); Smith, 110 S. Ct. at 2344 (Scalia, J., concurring).

in the underlying enterprise.[96] State tax cases cast courts in the "essentially legislative role of weighing the imponderable—balancing the importance of the state's interest in this or that . . . against the degree of impairment of commerce."[97] Courts are institutionally incapable of performing this role well. Moreover, even if they look exclusively at discrimination rather than at balancing it against state interests, they will struggle with the fact that state taxation "spans a spectrum ranging from the obviously discriminatory to the manipulative to the ambiguous to the wholly innocent."[98] Arbitrariness is unavoidable, but at least the standard based on laws that explicitly discriminate minimizes uncertainty by reaching only a well-defined class of cases. While the standard admittedly relies on purely formal distinctions and often fails to prevent intentional discrimination, he regards this failure as less damaging than the Court's plunge into legislative imponderables.[99] Justice Scalia would therefore leave to Congress the task of policing the more subtly discriminatory state taxes.[100]

Although Justice Scalia detests balancing, he implicitly does so in framing general rules of decision. To make his textual interpretation of the Constitution more palatable, he argues that the cost of his rule's lesser reach in barring undesirable state taxes is less than the benefit of its greater coherence and predictability. Schoettle would presumably argue to the contrary. One important variable in choosing between these positions is what Congress would do in the absence of active judicial oversight. If judicial review has discouraged Congress from handling the same range of problems more skillfully, there is all the more reason to agree with Justice Scalia; if Congress would not act, then only the courts can fill an arguable need. I turn to this and related questions of the politics of federalism in taxation in chapter 4, but first, given the constitutional issues Justice Scalia

---

[96]Tyler, 483 U.S. at 259–60 (Scalia, J., dissenting).

[97]Smith, 110 S. Ct. at 2344 (Scalia, J., concurring).

[98]Scheiner, 107 S. Ct. at 305 (Scalia, J., dissenting).

[99]See Scheiner, 107 S. Ct. at 305–06.

[100]Justice Scalia ignores the possibility that, if the Supreme Court announced the abolition of the negative commerce clause, Congress would immediately pass a statute barring discrimination against interstate commerce and instructing the Court to resume its prior role, now under the aegis of the positive commerce clause.

raises, I consider whether, as a matter of constitutional interpretation, the federal courts must follow one course or the other.

The Constitutional Grounds for Federal Judicial Review of State and Local Taxation

Judicial review of state and local taxes that affect outsiders or interstate commerce usually, though not exclusively, rests on the negative commerce clause—that ostensible though unstated corollary to the Constitution's explicit grant to Congress, through the "positive" commerce clause, of regulatory authority over interstate commerce. As Justice Scalia, echoing earlier commentators, has noted, the historical case for the negative commerce clause is unpersuasive. The text of the Constitution fails to mention it—contrary to what one might expect given its importance and in contradiction to drafting practices followed elsewhere in the Constitution.[101] Debate concerning enactment of the Constitution seems to have rested on the assumption that no negative commerce clause exists.[102] Arguably, the framers would not have adopted the Constitution had they understood the negative commerce clause to exist.[103] Finally, the original theoretical basis for the negative commerce clause—that the positive grant of authority over interstate commerce to Congress was meant to be exclusive, with the consequence that all state legislation in the area is in effect *ultra vires*—is historically and textually weak, has never been consistently followed by the courts, and could not be followed today without virtually eliminating states' power to legislate, given the breadth of the currently prevailing definition of "interstate commerce."[104]

This interpretation may counsel following Justice Scalia's lead and largely eliminating judicial review of state and local taxation, in the absence of congressional authorization. Yet counterarguments exist, on historical and other grounds. It may be significant, either

---

[101]See, for example, Currie, *The Constitution in the Supreme Court*, p. 173.

[102]See, for example, Scheiner, 107 S. Ct. at 264 (Scalia, J., dissenting); Felix Frankfurter, *The Commerce Clause under Marshall, Taney, and Waite* (Chapel Hill: University of North Carolina Press, 1937), p. 12.

[103]See, for example, Frankfurter, ibid., p. 19.

[104]See, for example, Scheiner, 107 S. Ct. at 261 (Scalia, J., dissenting).

for its own sake or as evidence of original intent, that the existence of a negative commerce clause was suggested as early as the 1820s, by Chief Justice Marshall in *Gibbons v. Ogden,* and has been with us ever since.[105] Moreover, the clause, even if a judicially created fiction, may perform the originally intended function of the import-export clause, which bars states from "lay[ing] any Imposts or Duties on Imports or Exports,"[106] if, as some have asserted, that clause was meant to apply to the interstate, not just international, movement of goods.[107] In addition, most commerce clause jurisprudence could probably continue to stand under plausible interpretations of the privilege and immunities, due process, or equal protection clauses.[108]

From a broader standpoint, we must consider how strictly we should feel bound by textualism and original intent. If doctrinal evolution to meet changing policy needs is methodologically permissible, this might be a particularly good place for it. An expansive negative commerce clause, if not quite uncontroversial, at least does not systematically favor some broad social groups against others; rather, it favors the whole against the parts, to collective long-term benefit.[109] It is also not identified with any particular point on the political spectrum. Thus, the rhetoric that portrays constitutional innovation as offensively political and countermajoritarian seems less applicable here.[110]

One could also powerfully argue unforeseen circumstances, if

---

[105]{{213}} 22 U.S. (9 Wheat.) 1, 209 (1824); see also Brown v. Maryland, 25 U.S. (12 Wheat.) 419, 448–49 (1827).

[106]Article I, section 10.

[107]See Harold W. Crosskey, *Politics and the Constitution in the History of the United States,* vol. 1 (Chicago: University of Chicago Press, 1953), pp. 295–323; Hellerstein, "State Taxation of Interstate Business," p. 39. The Supreme Court first held that the Import-Export Clause applies only to international commerce in Woodruff v. Parham, 75 U.S. (8 Wall.) 123 (1868).

[108]See Hellerstein, "State Taxation of Interstate Business," pp. 50–54, discussing overlap between negative commerce clause and other constitutional provisions.

[109]An expansive negative commerce clause may favor consumers and out-of-state producers over in-state producers, but everyone is a consumer and many in-state producers are also out-of-state producers elsewhere.

[110]See, for example, Robert Bork, *The Tempting of America* (New York: Free Press, 1990).

they are relevant under one's theory of constitutional interpretation.[111] The framers very likely failed to foresee the future growth either of interstate commerce or of state and local taxation. They may also have substantially overestimated the readiness of Congress to strike down state tax legislation hostile to interstate commerce.[112] That Congress never so acted during its first 180 years arguably suggests this.[113]

I conclude that the constitutional issue is sufficiently open to be decided on grounds of policy. From this perspective, the choice of a federal judicial standard involves a trade-off between the *benefits* of enhancing locational neutrality, which turn not only on an activist judicial standard's effectiveness but also on the burdens to interstate commerce that would otherwise be imposed by state and local governments and survive congressional oversight, and the *costs* of broad judicial enforcement, which potentially include not only rampant litigation and legal uncertainty but reduced benefit from the desirable exercise of state and local government authority. The following chapter examines the aspects of this trade-off that rely on an understanding of national or state and local politics.

---

[111]Aside from the question of whether the framers anticipated a "living Constitution" that would evolve to meet changing circumstances, there is the question of whether it makes sense to cling to their intent piecemeal when in so many complementary respects—relating, for example, to the scope of government activity—we have jettisoned their intent entirely.

[112]Political naiveté by the framers regarding Congress's willingness to strike down state laws burdening interstate commerce hardly seems implausible if one recalls, for example, their miscalculations relating to the Electoral College (including the belief that the college would perform an independent role and the failure to separate its vote for president from its vote for vice president), and their apparent belief, refuted within five years of the Constitution's adoption, that permanent political parties would not arise. On the latter, see Richard Hofstadter, *The Idea of a Party System: The Rise of Legitimate Opposition in the United States, 1780–1840* (Berkeley: University of California Press, 1969), pp. 53, 80.

[113]See Hellerstein and Hellerstein, *State and Local Taxation*, p. 324.

4

Political Factors Affecting the Practice of Federalism in Taxation

THE TRADE-OFF described at the end of the previous chapter turns in large part on questions about expected political behavior. In the absence of a federal judicial role, to what extent is Congress likely to overturn state provisions that burden interstate commerce or overtax nonresidents? Is the locational neutrality problem all that serious to begin with, given states' incentives to cooperate by promoting efficiency to their mutual advantage? Are there benefits to locating significant taxing authority at the state and local level that appear likely to outweigh the harm to locational neutrality? This chapter examines these questions in order.

Congress and the Political Efficacy of the "Positive" Commerce Clause

The framers counted on Congress, acting under the positive commerce clause, to restrain states' predilection to burden interstate commerce or export tax burdens to nonresidents.[1] The reliance seems a standard application of Madison's famous formula: "extend the sphere" of political action from the state to the national level to include more interests and thereby cure the vices of faction.[2] As it has turned out, however, Congress has almost never barred or restrained state and local taxes that created burden—even though judicial review of state and local taxation under

---

[1]See, for example, *Federalist* No. 42, p. 268, noting the "necessity of a superintending authority over the reciprocal trade of confederated States."

[2]See *Federalist* No. 10, p. 83.

the negative commerce clause does not make its role wholly redundant. In *Moorman* and *Commonwealth Edison,* for example, the Supreme Court not only upheld taxes with adverse effects on interstate commerce but also explicitly described these effects as properly considered by Congress, rather than the courts.[3]

It is therefore important to understand the reasons for Congress's pattern of inaction. If it would likely be taking a far more active role but for the federal courts' claim of jurisdiction, little might be lost by dispensing with the negative commerce clause. And it appears plausible that the courts' role at least marginally deters congressional action, even where a suspect tax is upheld. Once the Supreme Court becomes the primary filter for objectionable state and local taxes, its decision to let one stand may be (mis)interpreted politically as an affirmative endorsement or "clean bill of health." Moreover, without a regular congressional practice of reviewing such taxes, inertia may make reviewing the provisions that survive judicial scrutiny harder to overcome.

Despite this likely effect at the margin, there are powerful reasons for concluding that Congress would engage in little serious review of state and local taxes even without a negative commerce clause. Consider the basic flaw in Madison's "extend the sphere" solution to the problem of faction: the tendency of concentrated interests to be better organized and more aware of issues that affect them than diffuse interests are, leading to systematic transfers from the "many" to the "few."[4] This tendency inherently discourages an active congressional role in the state and local tax area, where a socially harmful provision often yields concentrated benefit (to the enacting state government and perhaps to in-state businesses) and diffuse harm (across the other forty-nine states and perhaps to in-state consumers).

To the extent that those harmed by a tax are sufficiently concentrated to be organized and aware of their interest, state political processes may already provide some protection. Concentrated interests need not include residents or voters to exert political influence.

---

[3]See Moorman Mfg. Corp. v. Blair, 437 U.S. 267, 280 (1978): "It is to [Congress], and not this Court, that the Constitution has committed . . . policy decisions [regarding income allocation rules]"; Commonwealth Edison v. Montana, 453 U.S. 609, 627 (1981): "The simple fact is that the appropriate level or rate of taxation is essentially a matter for legislative, and not judicial, resolution."

[4]See Olson, *The Logic of Collective Action*, p. 29.

The same financial and lobbying power that one generally needs to be effective before Congress may also apply at the state level. The ability to make campaign contributions, for example, may yield power everywhere. Thus, the congressional filter is somewhat duplicative, rather than independent or complementary, of the political filters in the states constraining enactment.

Even when a harmed outside interest group has greater influence in Congress than in the taxing state's legislature, the "extend the sphere" model is unlikely to work well in the state and local tax area. Madison counted on the inability of interest groups in a large and diverse polity to assemble majorities that would act together to invade others' rights or interests. Virtue, inertia, and what we would call the transaction costs of forming broad alliances offered a measure of protection.[5] In the state and local tax area, however, it is not enough for Congress to decline to erect trade barriers between the states. Rather, it must act affirmatively to bar the states from erecting barriers. Thus, the whole Madisonian structure of "checks and balances" impeding legislative action has the wrong effect here, where we need action, not inaction, to restrain the vices of faction.[6]

Recent scholarship in political science and law provides grounds for predicting congressional reluctance to strike down burdensome state and local taxes even when the forces demanding such action are quite strong. Assuming significant organized support for such taxes, Congress will typically face what Michael Hayes terms conflictual demand patterns. Hayes finds that Congress is reluctant to legislate when demand patterns are conflictual (even if the side demanding legislation is stronger), because of an "ungrateful electorate" that punishes legislation opposed to its preferences to a greater extent than it rewards legislation in favor.[7] Action is more visible than

---

[5]See *Federalist* No. 10, p. 83.

[6]While the framers may simply have missed this point or concluded that it had no good solution, some language in *The Federalist* could be read as supporting the view (under which the problem would not exist) that states lack the power to burden interstate commerce, perhaps because of the import-export clause rather than the negative commerce clause. See *Federalist* No. 7, pp. 62–63, noting that states would pursue conflicting and mutually injurious trade policies under a confederation but implying that they cannot under the Constitution; No. 42, pp. 267–68, stating that without the Constitution, states would be at liberty to regulate interstate commerce and load it with taxes on the import and export of goods.

[7]Michael Hayes, *Lobbyists and Legislators: A Theory of Political Markets* (New Brunswick, N.J.: Rutgers University Press, 1981), pp. 93–95.

inaction, and enemies have longer memories than friends, with the result that Congress usually tries to avoid conflictual issues altogether or defer their resolution to agencies and courts.[8] Jonathan Macey has shown that similar considerations often lead Congress to defer to state governments, ostensibly on grounds of principled federalism, instead of addressing issues that, from a public interest standpoint, might call for resolution at the national level.[9]

All this suggests that, in the absence of a negative commerce clause, Congress would be unwilling or unable to engage in much case-by-case review of questionable state and local taxes.[10] While the enactment of broad general rules to cover future disputes appears less unlikely, it has not happened so far, in large part because of the organized opposition of state and local governments.[11] Thus, if there is to be an effective check, it must probably be the courts—although one still could argue that such a check is worse than none at all.

State and Local Governments and the Need for a Commerce Clause

Despite congressional inability to monitor state and local taxation, there would be little need for a negative commerce clause if the states were not likely to impose significant relative burdens on each others'

---

[8]Ibid.; see also Morris P. Fiorina, "Legislative Choice of Regulatory Forms: Legal Process or Administrative Process?" *Public Choice* 39 (1982): 33, 55–57; Kenneth A. Shepsle, "The Strategy of Ambiguity: Uncertainty and Electoral Competition," *American Political Science Review* 66 (1972): 555; Peter H. Aranson, Ernest Gellhorn, and Glen O. Robinson, "A Theory of Legislative Delegation," *Cornell Law Review* (1983): 1, 33.

[9]Jonathan Macey, "Federal Deference to Local Regulators and the Economic Theory of Regulation: Toward a Public-Choice Explanation of Federalism," *Virginia Law Review* 76 (1990): 265.

[10]Under the Hayes-Macey analysis, Congress might, instead of doing nothing, reempower the federal courts to act under its positive commerce clause authority or establish an administrative agency (assuming this is constitutional) to perform the review function. Yet this would have largely the same effect as retaining the negative commerce clause, except insofar as (1) the empowering statute provided different (or at least clearer) directions to decision makers or (2) an agency acted differently from the courts, for example, by reason of its having independent investigative powers or being run by "experts."

[11]See, for example, Hellerstein and Hellerstein, *State and Local Taxation*, p. 325, describing an instance of interstate cooperation as designed to "stave off further Federal intervention."

citizens or businesses or on the act of crossing state boundaries. One might think that the states would refrain from imposing such burdens, given the general social gains from locational neutrality, the self-defeating nature of competition to impose greater burdens on others than others impose on oneself, and the capacity of threats of retaliation to enforce cooperation.[12] Unfortunately, however, while these considerations powerfully constrain state and local tax behavior and have created significant areas of cooperation, their force is incomplete.

Although the leading tax compacts and uniform allocation statutes receive far from universal adherence,[13] and while such adherence is motivated in part by the desire to forestall congressional intervention, interstate cooperation is in some respects impressive.[14] To give two examples, all states with broad-based personal income taxes grant credits for income taxes paid to other states with similar crediting provisions, and only Iowa fails to use a three-factor allocation formula for business income—although other states opportunistically vary the formula, for example, by giving greater weight to the sales factor in what are predominantly market states.[15]

Yet the history of Supreme Court commerce clause litigation richly testifies to the incompleteness of interstate cooperation. The important question is not whether existing cooperation is impressive and substantial but whether it is sufficient. The practical evidence of noncooperation from litigated cases—which evidence presumably would be even greater if states did not anticipate commerce clause challenges—accords with powerful theoretical reasons for expecting cooperation to fall well short of the optimum.

The sheer number of states and tax provisions creates significant monitoring and collective action problems. One state may be likely to benefit from enacting burden-exporting taxes even if some other

---

[12]See, for example, Kitch, "Regulation and the American Common Market," p. 14.

[13]The Multistate Tax Compact, developed in 1967, is currently subscribed to in full by only eighteen states, plus ten associate members. Hellerstein and Hellerstein, *State and Local Taxation*, p. 653. Likewise, only twenty-five states and the District of Columbia have substantially enacted the Uniform Division of Income for Tax Purposes Act. See ibid., p. 505.

[14]Comment by Walter Hellerstein in *Regulation, Federalism, and Interstate Commerce*, p. 124.

[15]See Hellerstein and Hellerstein, *State and Local Taxation*, pp. 968–69.

states (but not all) are watching its behavior and retaliating. States have differential opportunities to attempt to burden each other. States possessing scarce natural resources (like Montana in *Commonwealth Edison*) or a strategic location and national transportation networks (like Pennsylvania in *Scheiner*), for example, may be able to export more tax burdens to outsiders than outsiders can export back to them. Moreover, the role of concentrated interest groups within the states is extremely significant. A group in state X that can secure a tax benefiting itself at the expense of state Y need not be concerned about retaliation unless, first, the affected groups in state Y are sufficiently concentrated to act and, second, their retaliation against state X would hurt this very group (or other groups that are politically effective) rather than residents of state X generally. At the national level, it is well known that interest groups active in taxation tend to practice what Emil Schattschneider called "reciprocal noninterference," or agreeing to each other's favored tax concessions so long as each gets its own.[16] One would expect this pattern to hold even more powerfully at the state level, where opposing each others' special interest provisions might generally be more difficult and costly given the multiplicity of jurisdictions.

A further problem with state-level tax politics goes to tax exportation, which may benefit state political actors even if it is practiced sufficiently reciprocally to be, in fact, zero sum for all taxpayers and businesses. To understand why, we will digress briefly to a related question: why states would attempt to engage in tax exportation when they may not, as an economic matter, actually be accomplishing it. Consider the coal severance tax in *Commonwealth Edison*. While directly borne by consumers (predominantly from out of state), its real incidence, even in the short term, cannot be determined without examining such factors as

> the degree of geographic concentration, the mobility of various factors of industry, cartelization by taxing states, international competition or price-umbrella effects, natural substitutability, government regulation, the prevalence of

---

[16]See Shaviro, "Beyond Public Choice and Public Interest," p. 55 (and sources cited therein at n.254); Emil Schattschneider, *Politics, Pressures, and the Tariff: A Study of Free Private Enterprise in Pressure Politics, as Shown in the 1929–1930 Revision of the Tariff* (Hamden, Conn.: Anchor Books, 1935), pp. 135–36.

long-term contracts, the importance of transportation costs and the way in which such costs are determined, unionization, and market structure as well as the more mundane attributes of long- and short-run elasticities of supply and demand.[17]

In-state producers or landowners might bear most or all of the real tax burden. While Montana's willingness to levy the tax arguably suggests otherwise, on the theory that the enacting legislators or in-state interest groups must know better, one should not ascribe too much weight to their apparent judgment given the inherent difficulty of determining tax incidence.[18]

Imagine, however, that one is a Montana legislator considering voting to increase the coal severance tax dramatically and simultaneously to reduce the income and property taxes on local residents dramatically. (These changes were in fact made at the same time.)[19] To be confident of political gain from this vote, must one resolve the tax incidence question? While opposition from in-state interest groups, if any, may be significant, a yes vote brings an obvious political benefit regardless of the proposal's real effects on incidence—and even if it has no effects. The advantage is that, instead of being taxed visibly and directly, voters are now bearing tax burdens invisibly and indirectly. For politicians interested in popularity or reelection, perceived tax exportation is better than the real thing.

Perceived tax exportation is a particularly potent form of what Susan Hansen calls "fiscal illusion": the use of camouflage to pay for government without incurring voter wrath.[20] It is well documented that fiscal illusions can be quite resilient and that voter support for spending programs often depends on how well the costs of paying for the programs are disguised.[21] It follows that perceived tax exportation

---

[17]McLure, "Tax Exporting and the Commerce Clause," p. 171.

[18]The determination of tax incidence often baffles the most talented microeconomists who have studied it seriously, see ibid., p. 186; in other contexts, state legislatures also frequently get it wrong. See McLure, "The State Corporate Income Tax," pp. 341–42, suggesting that state corporate income taxes typically reflect progressive redistributional motives but are regressive in their actual incidence.

[19]See Epstein, "Taxation, Regulation, and Confiscation," p. 448.

[20]See Susan Hansen, *The Politics of Taxation: Revenue without Representation* (New York: Praeger Publishers, 1983), pp. 22–23, 35–36.

[21]See, for example, James Buchanan, *Public Finance in Democratic Process* (Chapel

is a valuable political tool for state legislators, permitting them to claim that they provide government services free, whether tax burdens actually are exported and whether other states respond by returning the favor.[22]

There is at least one more reason that state and local taxation tends to burden outsiders and interstate commerce notwithstanding the incentives to cooperate. As noted earlier, one of the principal costs of federalism in taxation goes to administration and compliance—arguably constituting "a drag on interstate trade almost as debilitating as the border restrictions our federal system was originally designed to prevent."[23] All jurisdictions would seemingly have an incentive to reduce these burdens, and surely to some extent they do. At the margin, however, no jurisdiction is likely to feel this incentive very strongly, given each jurisdiction's limited effect on nationwide costs of compliance and administration.

Moreover, while businesses would benefit from state (or federal) legislation reducing their compliance burdens, they are unlikely to lobby intensively for it. Collective action and free-rider problems inhibit such lobbying, not only absolutely but also relative to other lobbying. Here, the benefits of uniformity would be shared across a broad spectrum of multistate businesses. More targeted legislation— for example, creating industry-specific tax benefits—tends to induce greater cooperation and easier monitoring among affected businesses and to permit each such business to capture a greater share of the total benefit. Cooperation is also less likely because in many cases businesses do not want uniformity. Presumably, their goal is to reduce the sum of their tax payments and compliance costs, whereas

---

Hill: University of North Carolina Press, 1967), pp. 11–21; Hansen, ibid., pp. 109–11.

[22]Where tax exportation is successful, one could argue in its favor on efficiency grounds that the state's success in passing the cost to outsiders without reducing the quantity of goods exported suggests that the tax is on quasi-rents or pure profits, which in principle can be taxed without any distortive effect. Compare Rebecca Rudnick, "Corporate Tax Integration: Liquidity of Investment," *Tax Notes* 42 (Feb. 27, 1989): 1107, arguing on this ground that the classical double tax on equity-financed corporate income is not inefficient. Yet the perception argument above, unlike this argument, applies whether the attempted tax exportation is successful or not.

[23]See Henderson, "What We Can Do about What's Wrong with the Tax Law," p. 1352.

from a general social standpoint, to the extent that taxes are neutral transfers, the goal should be to reduce their compliance costs alone. Businesses may prefer socially costly locational disparity that permits them to reduce their tax bills—for example, through the exploitation of differences between states' income allocation rules or by inducing state tax competition to provide investment incentives.

While the costs of imposing disparate tax systems are likely to be undervalued by the various relevant actors, the real benefits to each jurisdiction of imposing the system it prefers are likely to be overestimated. It seems fair enough for legislatures that take different views of desirable tax policy to enact different types of taxes. Unfortunately, however, as I have discussed elsewhere in the context of the national legislature,

> In many cases, Congress legislates because its members and others who influence it value and benefit from the activity of legislating. The reasons for such behavior can be divided into two categories. First, proposing and enacting legislation is a means of symbolic communication with [poorly informed] members of the general public, of causing them to like a politician without the inconvenience (and possible political inconsequence) of actually having to benefit them tangibly. Thus, without regard to its actual effects, legislation can promote reelection. Second, succeeding legislatively is a means of exercising and demonstrating one's power. It is inherently gratifying (as when an emperor enjoys seeing statues of himself), and it increases one's prestige and status in political circles. Thus, without regard to its actual effects, legislation can promote self-interested goals apart from reelection.[24]

As a consequence of these incentives, the more separate actors have the opportunity to legislate, the more legislation there will be even without seriously held policy differences. In a federal system, for example, state as well as federal legislators may want to be able to say (to voters, each other, or themselves) that they have done something for the average taxpayer, the homeowner, the economy,

---

[24]Shaviro, "Beyond Public Choice and Public Interest," pp. 8–9. Compare comment by Walter Hellerstein in "Regulation, Federalism, and Interstate Commerce," p. 124.

education, or any other cause that momentarily seems salient and worthwhile. Legislatures may thus end up enacting differing rules that on balance impose tariff-like compliance and administrative burdens, simply because the members of each legislature value the opportunity to exercise their own discretion more than the total outcome (net of everyone's efforts) or nationwide uniformity.[25]

This observation can be generalized into a point about the Madisonian system of separation of powers, of which federalism is one application.[26] Instead of less legislation or even less costly legislation, the system may simply tend to produce less consistent and coherent legislation than a more unified and centralized system. Nonetheless, the system may be defended as a kind of "insurance" against the worst-case costs of centralized legislation that is consistent and coherent but thoroughly bad.[27] Does this defense, or any other, suggest that significant state-level autonomy in taxation, accompanied by limited or no review under the negative commerce clause, is a good idea despite the resulting harm to locational neutrality? The discussion below considers the principal forms that such an argument could take.

Preserving Broad State and Local Government Autonomy

So far, I have emphasized the benefits of large-scale rather than small-scale units of political decision making. Yet small political units, however ill-suited to advance locational neutrality, may have offsetting advantages of their own. Indeed, if this were not the case, large units would be so obviously and unambiguously superior that the debate over optimal size would never have become such a durable and popular genre in American political theory.[28]

---

[25]Consistently with this observation, in relatively nonpolitically salient areas, such as rules of evidence and commercial law, states tend to subscribe to uniform codes far more than in the area of taxation. Even in taxation, there are some uniformities, such as widespread "piggybacking," often with particular modifications, to the federal income tax code for state and local income tax purposes.

[26]See, for example, *Federalist* No. 51, p. 323.

[27]See Shaviro, "Beyond Public Choice and Public Interest," p. 106.

[28]See Deborah Stone, *Policy Paradox and Political Reason* (Glenview, Ill.: Scott, Foresman, 1988), pp. 296–97, noting the "optimal size" genre's long-standing popularity.

The principal arguments in favor of state and local government autonomy are as follows. First, in the tax context, it helps ensure that public goods (many of which are local rather than national in scope) will be provided and financed at the most efficient scale. Second, such autonomy promotes desirable tax competition between separate jurisdictions for residents and business investment, founded on the ease of exit by those dissatisfied with the trade-off between taxes paid and government services received. Third, even disregarding exit, small-scale government is more responsive to voters' preferences than large-scale government. Fourth, unfettered taxing powers permit state and local governments to exploit and develop the resources that they possess more readily, thus benefiting their residents and possibly promoting efficiency for much the same reason that private ownership of property is commonly thought efficient. Fifth, state and local autonomy has the Madisonian advantage of dividing political authority and thus reducing its capacity to do great harm. Sixth, such autonomy promotes experimentation by governments with different kinds of tax rules.

This section considers these arguments in turn and concludes that, in the tax area, they have some validity but relatively limited consequences. In particular, they suggest an important distinction. State and local discretion regarding the amount of revenue raised through taxes seems valuable and important despite its creating locational disparity. State and local discretion regarding exactly how revenue is raised seems generally less beneficial and thus more clearly ought to be minimized. Moreover, the narrower and less publicly salient the tax issue, the weaker the case for preserving discretion.

Benefits of Fiscal Federalism. While the multiunit federal structure of the United States is to some extent a historical accident reflecting its formation from separate colonies, good economic arguments support such a structure. The public goods that government provides often vary in their spatial incidence or in the scale at which they are most efficiently provided.[29] Assuming that a public good has

---

[29]See, for example, Musgrave and Musgrave, *Public Finance in Theory and Practice*, pp. 445–46; Gordon Tullock, "Federalism: Problems of Scale," *Public Choice* 6 (Spring 1969): 19.

no externalities outside its benefit region, concerns of efficiency suggest that the people in that region be exclusively responsible both for deciding whether to provide the good and for financing it. A larger-scale political unit may reduce government's responsiveness by giving influence over the decision to people who are not affected by it, or may make government too responsive by creating an incentive to seek public goods that are worth less to the beneficiaries than the amount society as a whole pays for the goods.[30]

These principles do not provide a perfect rationale for the existing practice of federalism in this country, given the extreme divergences between units of government and the scales of benefit from public goods. Jurisdictional lines are in many cases the arbitrary products of geography or history. Any attempt to draw the lines more rationally would be hampered by the unique scale of efficient provision or incidence of benefit of many public goods. Thus, even if otherwise feasible, perfect fiscal federalism would require, in Gordon Tullock's words, "a genuinely Rube Goldberg arrangement in which the individual citizen would be a member of a vast collection of governmental units, each . . . dealing with a separate activity."[31]

In practice, state and local governmental units are in some cases too small and in others too large to be optimally efficient in providing public goods. Moreover, positive and negative externalities surely abound from the provision of public goods within limited geographical units, reducing the validity of the entire model. Yet it nonetheless is plausible that dividing government into national, state, and local components brings us closer to the optimum than would a purely national system. A strong rationale therefore exists for having state and local governments decide what public goods to provide to their residents and take the responsibility for financing those public goods. Where different jurisdictions separately exercise discretion about

---

[30]Congressional pork-barrel legislation provides an instructive example. Such legislation, while formally provided at the national scale, may in fact be decided on locally—for example, by the House member who seeks a particular appropriation. Local decisions in the aggregate are then simply ratified at the national level through logrolling and are financed nationally, often leading to projects that are worth less to the beneficiaries than their cost to society. See, for example, Shaviro, "Beyond Public Choice and Public Interest," p. 38.

[31]Tullock, "Federalism: Problems of Scale," p. 25. Tullock notes that in a world with positive information costs this arrangement would be "very, very far from optimum" in practice, p. 26.

what public goods to finance, it becomes almost inevitable that they will levy taxes that differ in level or amount. This difference creates locational disparity in taxation that gives rise to some social costs, but the advantages of fiscal federalism may conceivably outweigh the costs.

All this discussion suggests that, on balance, it may be efficient for state and local jurisdictions to decide for themselves how much to raise in tax revenues. While it might also seem reasonable, without countervailing considerations, to let them decide what types of taxes to use, that does not follow as clearly from the fiscal federalism model (which would presumably suggest, if this were feasible, that residents pay for their precise share of the benefit from the public goods provided). And countervailing considerations plainly exist, since state or local discretion regarding the type of taxes levied increases the locational distortions already resulting from disparate levels of taxation and has the added drawback of encouraging tax exportation.

Without positive externalities from a jurisdiction's providing public goods, tax exportation is clearly inconsistent with fiscal federalism. Given that positive externalities frequently exist, however, one could argue that tax exportation is not objectionable after all.[32] This was essentially the Supreme Court's position in *Commonwealth Edison*, where it viewed Montana's exercise of police powers, thus maintaining local civilization to the benefit of all who passed through as justifying any degree of tax exportation, limited only by the requirement of nexus.[33]

Other than in failing to suggest any limit to tax exportation, the Court's argument may not be quite as preposterous as it initially appears. When not all beneficiaries from a public good must pay for it, there is a risk that it will be inefficiently undersupplied. Our confidence that Montana will remain a civilized society with roads and police even without tax exportation, however, minimizes this danger. At least up to a point, maintaining civilization is a public good likely to involve enormous consumer surplus. Many Montanans would presumably pay significantly higher taxes if necessary to fend

---

[32]Of course, if positive externalities are critical even for public goods whose principal incidence is local, the entire fiscal federalism model is called into question, but it is plausible that local decision makers are best suited to decide on and provide such goods.

[33]Commonwealth Edison v. Montana, 453 U.S. 609, 629 (1981).

off the collapse of their society (although some might choose instead to leave the state). Thus, the efficiency reason for affirmatively wanting to charge outsiders seems relatively unimportant, and standard economic notions of optimal taxation[34] suggest charging the least elastic revenue source—perhaps something pertaining to Montanans, if, as the principle condemning discrimination against interstate commerce implicitly posits, residency is less elastic than limited entry into a jurisdiction for commercial purposes.[35]

It seems clear that, when public goods are predominantly local in incidence, tax exportation tends to be undesirable, even with some positive externalities. While stronger substantive cases than Montana's for allowing tax exportation are easily imaginable, state and local governments have an incentive to engage in too much of it, not too little. Instances of significant benefit spillover can be addressed through action at the national level, cooperation between neighboring jurisdictions, and the charging of user fees for separable benefits provided to outsiders—for example, on roads that facilitate coal mining in Montana, establishing tolls that are reasonably commensurate with the roads' cost. When one adds together the costs of actual and perceived tax exportation and the other locational distortions, including administrative and compliance costs, that result when jurisdictions even "innocently" adopt different tax bases, it becomes clear that the case for state and local discretion regarding the types of taxes used is weaker than the case for such discretion regarding the amount of revenue raised through taxes.

The Tiebout and Tax Competition Models. In public finance theory, even advocates of a relatively large government role commonly acknowledge the difficulty of calibrating taxes and expenditures to people's preferences as efficiently as well-functioning private markets make possible.[36] This difficulty persists even under optimal fiscal federalism. Governments have local power monopolies, public goods

---

[34]See, for example, Hettich and Winer, "Blueprints and Pathways," p. 428, describing the optimal taxation norm that "activities or commodities for which substitution effects are the smallest ought to be taxed more heavily."

[35]See chapter 3, section entitled "Why Bar Discrimination While Permitting Other Locational Disparity?"

[36]See, for example, Paul Samuelson, "The Pure Theory of Public Expenditures," *Review of Economics and Statistics* 36 (1954): 387, 388–89.

cannot be sold separately just to people who want them, and voting is too crude to disaggregate particular preferences or register their intensity. Charles Tiebout, however, argued in a celebrated article that localizing the scale of government where feasible makes possible a market-style solution to the problem of satisfying voters' preferences in the public sector. If numerous small-scale jurisdictions offer distinctive tax and service packages, if people are sufficiently aware of the different packages available, and if exit from one jurisdiction to another is sufficiently cheap (among other necessary preconditions), then the various jurisdictions will in effect compete for residents in much the same way that private businesses compete for customers.[37] Small scale is critical to Tiebout's analysis because it tends to make exit cheaper and permits the existence of a greater number of choices.

Tiebout's analysis parallels the traditional wisdom that federalism promotes tax competition among the states, since overtaxation induces exit or reluctance to enter.[38] Under this view, taxation is seen purely as a cost to businesses or individuals of locating or remaining in a particular jurisdiction, devoid of offsetting benefits at the margin from added spending. Accordingly, taxpayers' ability to flee encourages a desirable "race to the bottom" in levels of taxation or at least inhibits an undesirable "race to the top."

The two related models can be challenged in a number of respects, however. First, they may expect too much from the exit option. Exit is often costly. For individuals, even beyond the direct costs of a move (including information and search costs), the decision to "vote with one's feet" may be discouraged by personal attachments to particular areas and by geographically limited job or housing opportunities. Businesses not only must consider a wide range of nontax factors in deciding where to invest but also, once located, may be unable to move without sacrificing fixed investments, ranging from physical plant to goodwill.[39] To the extent that exit is prohibi-

---

[37]Tiebout, "A Pure Theory of Local Expenditures." Tiebout's jurisdictions are not trying to maximize the number of residents but to achieve the optimal scale.

[38]See, for example, Macey, "Federal Deference to Local Regulators," p. 291, noting the "traditional defense of a strong federalist system as a device for achieving a more efficient legal system by encouraging competition among the states."

[39]A business may also incur the cost of preserving its future mobility by keeping its capital in mobile form where, exit considerations aside, creating immobile capital would be more profitable.

tively costly, the benefits of the Tiebout and tax competition models are lost. To the extent that exit is costly but still done, the costs incurred yield a social loss, reducing or even eliminating the net social benefit predicted by the models. Put differently, locational disparity still has costs even if it also has benefits.

A second problem with the Tiebout and tax competition models is that the information needed for their effective functioning may not be available. Recent studies suggest that, even in urban areas containing a multiplicity of local governments—seemingly ideal settings for the Tiebout model—voters typically lack sufficient information about alternative tax and service packages to make the kinds of decisions that Tiebout posits.[40] The vast diversity that is currently tolerated between jurisdictions' tax systems surely contributes to this problem. Prospective residents would find it easier to compare tax packages that were more similarly structured and differed principally in tax rates. The existing structural diversity leads, perhaps intentionally, to information overload.

In addition, the diversity that creates this information overload yields few offsetting advantages. One of the most attractive features of the Tiebout model—its promise of diversity in the packages offered to suit diversity in people's tastes—has been questioned empirically. It appears that the greatest differences in jurisdictions' spending patterns result, not from whether local voters prefer, say, art museums or swimming pools, but instead from differences in fiscal capacity.[41] Differences in spending on education between jurisdictions with similar proportions of children, for example, vary principally with wealth rather than with voters' taste for spending on education.[42]

---

[40]See David Lowery and William E. Lyons, "The Impact of Jurisdictional Boundaries: An Individual-Level Test of the Tiebout Model," *Journal of Politics* 51 (1989): 73. Businesses, because of advantages of scale, may be more likely to have relevant information about tax levels, but even they may be unable to predict the future levels of taxation that will apply to fixed investments.

[41]See Richard Briffault, "Our Localism," *Columbia Law Review* 90 (1990): 1, 422–25.

[42]Some jurisdictions may specialize either in providing good public schools or in having low taxes, thus encouraging geographical sorting between parents of school-age children and others. Yet this example of Tiebout-style behavior is in large part an artifact of the federal income tax system, which denies deductions for the costs of sending one's children to private schools but allows deductions for real property

83

Reliance on diversity in preferences appears even less appropriate for issues of taxation. Given people's varying preferences, diversity may be valuable with regard to a jurisdiction's choice to be high tax and high service or low tax and low service. Yet the same may not be as true with regard to the choice of how to raise a particular amount of revenue. Services are provided in kind and therefore may vary sharply in subjective value depending on one's taste, but taxes are paid in the invariant form of cash. Thus, to the extent that people care principally about their own taxes, it seems doubtful that they will often be much concerned about what types of taxes they are paying (other than in preferring low compliance costs), holding the amount that they pay constant.[43]

Moreover, to the extent that people care about the allocation of tax burdens within the jurisdiction as a whole, the Tiebout and tax competition models suggest an inherent problem with attempting to provide diversity at the local level.[44] Assume that voters differ in their attitudes toward progressive taxes that redistribute wealth. Even if the voters who favor such taxes concentrate in particular jurisdictions, they cannot realize their preference unless suitable targets of redistributive taxation consent to live in those jurisdictions.[45] Wealthy taxpayers and holders of capital—the most likely and plausible

---

taxes that are used to finance public education (a distortion that could be addressed by changing either of the two rules). Such specialization may also respond opportunistically to the exit costs that prevent some nonparents from leaving high-tax, good-school jurisdictions, thereby making such persons subsidize a benefit that, even if partly a public good, primarily benefits its direct recipients.

[43]Even where people manifest strong aversion to one particular type of tax—as in Connecticut currently, where Governor Weicker's push for an income tax has aroused strong opposition—popular sentiment may rest in large part on the belief that enacting the unpopular tax would cause total taxes to increase, at least over the long term. Note that, just as creating a new income tax in addition to the sales tax is unpopular in Connecticut, so at the national level enacting a sales (or value-added) tax in addition to the sales tax is unpopular. Many attribute Ways and Means Chairman Albert Ullman's electoral defeat in 1980 to his advocacy of a national value-added tax.

[44]People may also care about the policy arguments aside from incidence for different taxes, an issue that I discuss in chapter 4, section entitled "Preserving Broad State and Local Government Autonomy."

[45]If I want to redistribute my own wealth, I can make voluntary contributions to suitable persons or causes and do not need the tax system's assistance.

targets of redistributive taxation—are precisely the ones most likely to enjoy high mobility.[46]

This raises a normatively controversial aspect of the Tiebout and tax competition models. Assume that "conservatives" favor a small government sector, little or no wealth redistribution, and favorable tax treatment for capital, while "liberals" favor a large government sector, significant wealth redistribution, and high taxes on capital. Under these assumptions, conservatives but not liberals will like the consequences for progressivity of cheap exit.[47]

Yet each side has its own countervailing considerations. First, both may be dismayed by the inefficiency of departures from locational neutrality. Moreover, in a country where support at the national level for tax progressivity and redistribution is at most "weak and ambivalent,"[48] highly liberal policies may be most likely to prevail politically at smaller-scale jurisdictions that diverge from the mainstream (although highly progressive taxation may be ineffective at the local level given the ease of exit).[49] This may in some instances make liberals friends, and conservatives foes, of state and local discretion in the tax area.[50] Another consideration is that the exportation of perceived or actual tax burdens to nonvoters may be most feasible at the state and local level, where only one state's voters are represented and the amount of market power being wielded is likely smaller than at the national level. This may favor the liberal objective of promoting high taxation and spending, but liberals may disapprove of the lack of taxpayer consent or the taxes' incidence.

---

[46]See, for example, Briffault, "Our Localism," p. 420.

[47]See, for example, Paul E. Peterson, *City Limits* (Chicago: University of Chicago Press, 1981); Karen Orren, *Corporate Power and Social Change* (New York: Cambridge University Press, 1974).

[48]John Witte, *The Politics and Development of the Federal Income Tax* (Madison: University of Wisconsin Press, 1985), p. 352.

[49]The same may be true of highly conservative policies that diverge from the mainstream, but the point is that, in the area of tax progressivity, the mainstream tilts to the conservative side. The reverse may be true in other areas, such as abortion policy, where tight restrictions (typically a "conservative" position), if constitutionally permitted, might be most likely to prevail in selected states and localities.

[50]See Stone, *Policy Paradox and Political Reason*, p. 304, arguing that support for making decisions at a particular level in the federal system typically reflects "a belief that some particular interest is stronger in a particular arena."

85

Finally and most important, the question presented is not whether taxation should be exclusively national or exclusively state and local. Continuing national taxation is a given. Moreover, since the argument for state and local discretion regarding the amount of tax levied is relatively strong, consider focusing on discretion regarding the types of taxes used. Given the potential for perceived tax exportation and the greater mobility of the wealthy and of capital, the dominant effect of such discretion may be to increase the net amount of state and local taxation (and thus the size of government) but to make such taxation less progressive. The result could be the worst of both worlds: the inefficiency many conservatives abhor[51] without the redistribution many liberals favor.[52]

Greater Responsiveness of Small Government Units. A further possible advantage of smaller government units is that they may be more responsive to the policy preferences of local voters.[53] In smaller units, each individual's vote counts for relatively more, there may be greater internal homogeneity and thus agreement, a sense of community participation may be easier to foster,[54] and, as even James Madison (while generally preferring the larger scale) admitted, government officials may be more familiar with local sentiments and conditions.[55] These considerations plainly strengthen the case for state and local control over taxation. Once again, however, they apply more forcefully to the amount of tax levied than to the types of taxes used.

---

[51]Liberals, of course, should and often do oppose inefficiency, but it is often less prominent in their rhetoric.

[52]This suggests that at least certain liberals and conservatives (those who disagree mainly about the merits of what is often called the "equity versus efficiency" trade-off posed by an increase in the size of government) should agree that state-level discretion in the tax area should be reduced. Yet American politics, or, for that matter, the Supreme Court, reaches no such consensus. If anything, a consensus to preserve such discretion prevails. I suspect that liberals and conservatives alike tend to cherish the existence of multiple levels of political discretion because it increases the chance that they will enjoy the satisfaction of prevailing somewhere, albeit the real effects of prevailing anywhere are reduced.

[53]See, for example, McConnell, "Federalism: Evaluating the Founders' Design," p. 1493.

[54]See, for example, *Federalist* No. 10; Gerald E. Frug, "Empowering Cities in a Federal System," *Urban Lawyer* 19 (1987): 553.

[55]See *Federalist* No. 10, p. 83.

Given fiscal illusion, popular understanding of the amount of taxation imposed by a jurisdiction and its relationship to the value of government services provided can be disappointingly limited.[56] Yet it often functions as a powerful constraint—for example, causing the defeat of politicians who enact or threaten unwanted tax increases.[57] Thus, for amount-of-tax issues, the argument that people will get more of what they want if more control remains at the state and local levels has some force. For type-of-tax issues, however, it appears considerably less persuasive.

Voters may care about what types of taxes their jurisdictions use for reasons for incidence or effect. We have already seen, however, that issues of tax incidence are poorly understood by voters (and even economists), with the result that support for particular taxes often depends on questionable or downright erroneous factual premises. Consider, for example, state-level corporate income taxes, which probably gain much of their political support from the apparently erroneous belief that they are borne by shareholders, rather than by employees and consumers.[58] We have also seen that control over incidence is impeded at the state and local level by the relative ease of exit by targets of redistribution and that control can be misused to export tax burdens to persons neither participating as voters nor benefiting significantly from the jurisdiction's spending. The social gain from maximizing state and local-level voter control over tax incidence therefore appears relatively weak.

Taxes not only raise revenue but also function as regulation. The choice between a sales tax and an income tax, for example, may affect saving, and the decision to grant homeowners a tax preference may affect home ownership.[59] Voters in different jurisdictions may

---

[56]Thus, the demand for public goods often depends on how visibly they are financed rather than on their cost, and many people apparently believe that government services can be provided for free. See, for example, Buchanan, *Public Finance in Democratic Process*, pp. 11–12; Hansen, *The Politics of Taxation*, p. 262.

[57]Recent examples include the defeat of Walter Mondale in the 1984 presidential election after he promised a tax increase, the defeat of Senator Dole in the 1988 New Hampshire Republican presidential primary after he failed to "take the pledge" not to raise taxes, and the 1981 state legislative elections in New Jersey, where the Democrats were overwhelmingly defeated after Governor Florio increased taxes.

[58]See McLure, "The State Corporate Income Tax," pp. 341–42.

[59]See chapter 2, section entitled "The Definition of a Tax and Its Significance for Locational Neutrality."

want different regulatory effects for themselves, and while in some cases their efforts may simply offset each other, in others the resulting differentiation might increase aggregate satisfaction.

The problem with supporting broad state and local discretion on this ground is that, while taxes are only one type of regulation, they are a type that voters poorly understand. For a variety of reasons, including the simple dislike of taxation, people tend to assess regulatory uses of the tax system less rigorously than regulation by many other means.[60] Thus, to limit state and local discretion in the tax area would not be sufficiently broad to prevent regulation where desired, because alternative means to regulatory ends will usually exist; nor would it be so formalistic and easily evaded as to serve no purpose, in that the alternative means might be more likely than tax provisions to receive meaningful political scrutiny.[61] Accordingly, the responsiveness argument for preserving state and local control over the types of taxes levied, while not completely without force, is plausibly outweighed by the arguments for greater uniformity and centralized control over state and local tax bases.

One could argue that tax issues in general—the amount of tax levied aside—are too poorly understood for increasing our political system's aggregate responsiveness to voter preferences to have much value. Certainly, many observers of the political process behind the federal income tax have concluded that responsiveness commonly fails to yield not only a fair or efficient tax system but even one satisfying to the voters whose preferences it ostensibly reflects.[62] Without pushing this argument too far, it seems clear that for some types of tax issues—in particular, those too narrow or esoteric to attract widespread attention and concern—political responsiveness has relatively little value.

---

[60]See Shaviro, "Beyond Public Choice and Public Interest," pp. 62–63. This is not to deny that some other forms of regulation—such as keeping social programs off-budget by requiring businesses to provide specified services—may be judged with a similar lack of rigor.

[61]Similarly, a well-known argument in the context of the federal income tax system holds that the extensive use of "tax expenditures" is undesirable for structural political reasons. See, for example, Surrey, *Pathways to Tax Reform*.

[62]See, for example, Witte, *The Politics and Development of the Federal Income Tax*; Shaviro, "Beyond Public Choice and Public Interest," pp. 63–64; Stanley Surrey, "The Congress and the Tax Lobbyist—How Special Tax Provisions Get Enacted," *Harvard Law Review* 70 (1957): 1145.

Compare, for example, choosing income tax depreciation schedules with choosing between an income tax and a sales tax to raise the bulk of a state's revenue. The depreciation schedule is far less salient than the choice of tax, and thus the power to control that issue locally seems unlikely to affect directly, to any significant extent, public satisfaction. By contrast, voters across the country frequently express interest in the choice between an income tax and a sales tax (as Connecticut's Governor Weicker has recently learned).[63] However skeptical one is of the underlying public understanding of each tax's incidence and effects, it is difficult to argue that when voters express a preference for one type of tax over another they are mistaken about what they truly prefer. Even if their preference is based on erroneous factual premises—meaning that they are asking to live in a fool's paradise—acceding to the preference might still yield the highest attainable public satisfaction, assuming that the public's ignorance cannot be remedied. After all, a sense of satisfaction is no less subjectively real for being founded on illusion.[64]

Again, however, the fool's paradise argument for state and local autonomy in taxation reaches only those issues that are sufficiently salient to evoke strongly held opinions on a broad scale. For the narrow and esoteric issues that are most common in the tax area—generally, those of tax-base design as opposed to the choice between well-known types of tax base—the case for greater uniformity and centralized control remains strong.

Statewide Control over Resources and the Efficiency Gains from Monopoly. One of the consequences of broad state and local government autonomy in taxation is that it affords particular jurisdictions the opportunity to exploit their natural or other resources. Montana, for example, can use the coal severance tax to extract a higher price for its coal, assuming that its market power is in fact

---

[63]See, for example, Kirk Johnson, "Budget Is Passed for Connecticut with Income Tax," *New York Times*, August 23, 1991; Kirk Johnson, "Effort to Repeal Income Tax Fails in Hartford," *New York Times*, December 14, 1991.

[64]In endorsing the "fool's paradise," I argue, for the moment, against the procentralization theme of this article. The reader who disagrees with me about the fool's paradise should conclude that the case for increased centralization is even stronger than I recognize and thus should be moved in the direction of greater rather than lesser agreement with my general conclusions.

sufficient to raise the aftertax price paid by out-of-state customers. Similarly, Pennsylvania can attempt to exploit its highly strategic geographical location if it permits levies such as the one in *Scheiner*,[65] and New York City and Florida can use hotel taxes to exploit their attractiveness as tourist destinations.[66] The presumably intended effect in each case is not so much to tax in-state resource owners as to raise the aftertax prices paid by outsiders. In effect, states form cartels within their borders that individual owners of coal mines, hotels, and the like would be unable to organize, given collective action problems and the antitrust laws, and the states then appropriate the monopoly profits to themselves.

If this does not sound like an argument in favor of state and local government autonomy in taxation, it can be converted into one by adding the assertion that the residents of the taxing states *ought* to be able to exploit their resources to their profit. This assertion can be defended either as a matter of entitlement or on efficiency grounds.

The entitlement argument—for example, that Montanans ought to reap maximum benefit from Montana's coal—is relatively easy to answer. While "Montana for the Montanans" may sound, as a base line matter of justice, no less plausible than "Montana for the benefit of all Americans" or "Montana for the benefit of all humanity," in practice it has disadvantages. When all states attempt to exploit their particular advantages at the expense of those in other states by organizing in-state monopolies, society as a whole is left worse off, because of the well-known dead-weight welfare triangle loss that monopoly causes.[67] Thus, behind a veil of ignorance all states would

---

[65]Recently, while traveling through Pennsylvania after having been warned that the state rigorously enforces its fifty-five-mile-per-hour speed limit, I conjectured that this was one more example of an attempt to export taxes and burden interstate commerce. A large proportion of the speeding fines levied in Pennsylvania no doubt are paid by outsiders, who may tend to be less familiar with the state's policy and to have long distances to travel (increasing the urge to travel fast). As is often the case with public choice explanations, however, this one proved difficult to verify. I observed that Pennsylvania also seemed to make greater-than-normal use of speed bumps and signs warning motorists to reduce their speed, perhaps evidencing a culture of traffic safety independent of tax exportation.

[66]See Wade, "Tax Collectors Lean on the Out-of-Towners."

[67]See, for example, Ryan C. Amacher and Holley H. Ulbrich, *Principles of Economics*, 4th ed. (Cincinnati: South-Western Publishing Co., 1989), p. 519.

90

presumably agree, and arguably by adopting the Constitution they did agree, mutually to forgo the advantages of being able to use taxation to extract monopoly profits from their resources.

The state's monopoly power, however, eliminates not only the fortuitous collective action problem that inhibits seekers of monopoly profit but also the regrettable collective action problem that inhibits those who would like to develop a state's resources more fully. Assume, for example, that the infrastructure needed by New York to support a thriving tourist industry would not be built or maintained unless its costs can be charged to tourists and that public good and collective action problems prevent anyone other than the government, through taxes, from collecting the amounts that are needed.

The argument is a standard one about the welfare advantages of monopoly, as well as collective or public ownership of property.[68] It is also identical in form to the standard argument for allowing private property by granting the owner monopoly rights over a particular asset—namely, that by internalizing to owners the social benefits from the property, we can induce them to use and develop the property to maximum social advantage.[69] For both monopoly and private property rights, the assessment requires comparing benefits of internalization with harms, such as the welfare triangle loss, across a broad spectrum. While such an assessment is beyond the scope of this volume, the standard wisdom over the years has been that for private property the benefits outweigh the harms, while for monopoly the harms are greater. This assessment certainly seems plausible in the context of state and local taxes, where only rarely does it seem likely that the tax revenues extracted from outsiders are needed and would be used for desirable infrastructure that would not otherwise exist because of collective action problems.

---

[68]Joseph Schumpeter, *Capitalism, Socialism, and Democracy*, 2d ed. (New York: Harper & Brothers, 1942), pp. 81–82; and J. Kenneth Galbraith, *American Capitalism*, 2d ed. (Boston: Houghton Mifflin, 1956), argue that monopoly increases business innovation by ensuring that none of the gains from innovation will be captured by imitative competitors. The available empirical evidence about innovation essentially refutes that argument, however. See Amacher and Ulbrich, p. 563.

[69]See, for example, Harold Demsetz, "Toward a Theory of Property Rights," *American Economic Review: Proceedings and Papers* 57 (1967); Cass Sunstein, "On Property and Constitutionalism" (Chicago Law and Economics Working Paper No. 3, 2d Series, 1991), p. 6.

Decentralizing Authority over Taxation. A further argument for broad state and local government discretion in matters of taxation is the standard Madisonian separation-of-powers view, under which the creation of multiple independent authorities reduces the harms feared from vigorous government. Here again the argument is not completely without force but seems of relatively minor import. In particular, state and local governments cannot directly constrain the exercise of federal taxing authority and thereby prevent "tyranny." Thus, their only separation-of-powers benefit is to make national tax policy as a whole less consistent and coherent—a benefit that, while conceivably desirable if one is sufficiently pessimistic about such policy, has significant costs.

The fact that control over taxes at the state and local levels is in addition to, not a potential substitute for, control over taxes at the national level is important for more than the standard Madisonian reasons. It largely eliminates the relevance of any claim that tax base standardization is a mistake because national authorities are unlikely to make better decisions than local authorities. Whether that claim is factually correct is debatable, given the greater number of represented interests and the reduction of incentives for interstate tax exportation at the national level. The claim nonetheless is not clearly wrong: a glance at the Internal Revenue Code shows that it is rife with special interest provisions, often (as with oil and gas tax preferences) betraying a regional bias. Yet the relative merits of localized and national decision making are not decisive when the question presented is to what extent we should have "one of the most undesirable outcomes in a federal system—dual state and federal regulation of the same subject matter," leading at a minimum to higher costs of tax compliance and administration.[70]

Promoting Experimentation. A final argument for broad state and local autonomy in the tax area is that it facilitates governmental experimentation. When there are more separate units controlling their own tax systems, not only can a greater number of different ideas be tried but also each experiment involves less aggregate social risk than if it were attempted nationwide. Therefore, a decentralized federal system ostensibly promotes a pace of intellectual progress in

---

[70]Kitch, "Regulation and the American Common Market," p. 47.

92

matters of tax policy that would not otherwise be possible.[71]

This argument is powerful to the extent that tax politics is an orderly, rational process in which the principal (or a major) impediment to developing good law is simply the lack of hard empirical knowledge. Under the skeptical view of tax politics that I and many others have taken, however, the case for promoting experimentation loses most of its force.[72] Given the inherent difficulty of establishing causal relationships between provisions that are enacted and subsequent social effects, "experiments" often have surprisingly little evidentiary value.[73] Moreover, what value there is tends not to be examined very cogently. Consider the national experiment of the early 1980s with greatly expanded tax incentives to promote saving and investment, which was followed by a sharp decline in national saving and investment (although arguably for unrelated reasons) but which has failed to dismay or even compel much explanation from those who advocate restoring these incentives.[74] Given both interest group politics and politicians' incentives to seek salient and dramatic legislation as an end in itself, the experiments are not being conducted by reliable "scientists."[75] Even the lessons that are learned may be the wrong ones, such as what types of provisions are effective in disadvantaging outside businesses or creating perceived tax exportation.

The rhetorically appealing metaphor of a national "laboratory" where state and local governments conduct valuable experiments that, when successful, can be emulated elsewhere, is surely not entirely without foundation. Yet as one surveys the area that this

---

[71]Compare McConnell, "Federalism: Evaluating the Founders' Design," p. 1498.

[72]See, for example, James Buchanan and Robert Wagner, *Democracy in Deficit: The Political Legacy of Lord Keynes* (San Diego: Academic Press, 1977), pp. 129–34; Hansen, *The Politics of Taxation*, p. 243; Schattschneider, *Politics, Pressures, and the Tariff*, p. 239; Shaviro, "Beyond Public Choice and Public Interest,"; Surrey, "The Congress and the Tax Lobbyist"; Witte, *The Politics and Development of the Federal Income Tax.*

[73]Compare Daniel Shaviro, "Exchange on Public Choice," *University of Chicago Law Review* 57 (1990): 834.

[74]While the tax incentives of the early 1980s have not, for the most part, been restored as yet, this may be more because of budgetary considerations than evidence suggesting that the incentives were ineffective. See Shaviro, "Beyond Public Choice and Public Interest," pp. 52–53.

[75]See ibid., pp. 8–9.

metaphor describes—for example, the 7,000 separate sales tax jurisdictions and the forty-odd state personal and business income taxes, each with its own array of provisions—and reflects on the real but often invisible consequences, both substantive and administrative, of so much diversity, it is hard to remain confident that the "laboratory" is yielding an acceptable ratio of benefit to cost. The case for moving at least some distance in the direction of nationally imposed uniformity remains compelling.

In summary, while state and local governments serve a number of important purposes, the case for preserving their discretion in deciding what to tax (as opposed to how much to tax) seems weak. Even if problems such as administrative complexity and breakdowns in interstate cooperation are no more serious in the tax area than elsewhere, the offsetting benefits of localized control seem inadequate. This seems particularly true for relatively narrow and esoteric tax issues, such as the design details for a particular tax base.

In principle, one might even want to establish a uniform tax base that all state and local jurisdictions were required to use when levying taxes and allow them discretion only regarding the rate. Yet such a course would not only be politically implausible and constitutionally suspect—even Congress's modern commerce clause powers may not reach that far—but have significant disadvantages.[76] Reliance on a single uniform tax base would tend to make state and local tax revenues overly subject to fluctuation. Using a variety of bases serves as a kind of insurance, reducing the likely revenue effects of any particular kind of economic change; moreover, it permits marginal rates to be lower across the spectrum, thus reducing the distortive effects of any one base. Chapter 5 incorporates this constraint, along with the stronger arguments for preserving state and local autonomy, into the development of specific recommendations for changing the current practice of federalism in taxation.

---

[76]Depriving the states of all authority over taxation, other than that concerning the rate applied to a single uniform base, might be too far removed from the framers' expectations regarding state-federal relations to survive constitutional scrutiny. See, for example, *Federalist* Nos. 32, 33.

5
Conclusions and Recommendations

So FAR, this book has reached the following main conclusions:

• A principle opposing tariffs within U.S. borders seems not only substantively correct but also politically, historically, and constitutionally uncontroversial. The best argument for this principle is that tariffs impair locational neutrality. Tariffs are not unique in this regard, however, and locational neutrality almost inevitably suffers if state and local governments have authority over taxation.

• Since complete locational neutrality is unattainable in a federal system (and not even desirable given considerations of fiscal federalism), some narrower principle must be used by courts charged with determining which state and local taxes are impermissible. In this context, the case for a principle barring discrimination against outsiders and interstate commerce is plausible, although not overwhelming. While such a principle may not reach all the cases in which one would like to intervene, it serves a valuable function to the extent that it facilitates line drawing and filters out the very worst state and local taxes. Yet in these respects, the antidiscrimination principle has worked poorly in practice, because of its theoretical limitations and the courts' implicit balancing of it against the positive value ascribed to the autonomy of state and local government.

• At neither the national nor the state and local level are ordinary political processes likely to keep the harm to locational neutrality within acceptable bounds. Arguments that the state and local political process serves important purposes, outweighing the harm to locational neutrality, are persuasive with regard to levels of taxation but not with regard to tax-base design, particularly in light of the resulting administrative costs and the incentives for actual or per-

95

ceived tax exportation. Therefore, we may want to limit discretion of state and local governments to specify tax bases, while permitting them to set the tax rates that apply to acceptable bases.

These conclusions have strong positive implications for both Congress and the federal courts. At least some congressional action seems desirable because it can take the form of coherent rules, based on contextual policy considerations, that no one need pretend the Constitution mandates. Even if judges are intellectually capable of prescribing better rules than legislators—despite the handicaps of addressing only the cases that arise and hearing principally from adversaries with narrow litigating interests—they may conclude with some justification that their role does not extend to specifying precise rules that may look arbitrary and political. Moreover, while there is little reason to expect congressional intervention in specific disputes as they arise, it is less implausible that Congress will enact general rules to govern future disputes as yet unknown. I therefore consider what Congress should do before I turn to the federal courts.

An important countervailing consideration, however, is the possible danger of involving Congress on a continuing basis in specifying state and local tax bases. Regular involvement might spur Congress, in response to interest group pressures, to give away potential state and local revenue, unconstrained by the budgetary concerns that it has when it considers the effect of tax rules on the national budget. Accordingly, even when Congress can specify detailed rules that would improve state and local taxation, it should exercise caution, unless it can explain such rules as one-time legislation predicated on creating uniformity for its own sake.[1]

The dangers and unlikelihood of congressional involvement suggest that many of the rules discussed below should instead be implemented by the states themselves. Obviously, the difficulties of

---

[1] The preferred model for congressional action would be that of policy entrepreneurship, overcoming political inertia by selling an attractive and simple idea to the general public, or at least the Washington political community, over the heads of the most narrowly interested parties. Similar dynamics have led in the past to federal income tax reform, deregulation of such industries as trucking and the airlines, and regulatory legislation addressing air and water pollution, automobile safety, consumer product safety, and racial discrimination. Legislation too detailed and political in appearance to fit this model may be undesirable because it would invite continual tinkering by Congress.

coordinating and monitoring cooperation among fifty separate actors, along with the political difficulty for any one state to sacrifice voter or politician preferences for diversity (even where such sacrifice is well worth the reciprocal sacrifices by other states), can be expected to limit progress. Yet the states might collectively benefit from informal and at least nominally apolitical institutions to promote cooperation by suggesting uniform rules that many or all might agree to follow. This device has worked, if imperfectly, in the past. As an example, the Uniform Division of Income for Tax Purposes Act, currently subscribed to by twenty-five states and the District of Columbia, was promulgated at an annual meeting of the National Conference of Commissioners on Uniform State Laws.[2]

Congress

The steps that Congress ought to consider taking can be arrayed in three groups. I will discuss each, in order of increasing ambitiousness, and then consider whether any exceed the constitutional limits to Congress's power over the states.

Coordinating State and Local Tax Bases. Perhaps the least controversial proposal is to require the states to use uniform apportionment rules in dividing among themselves tax bases of potentially national scope, such as income or sales. In particular, a uniform apportionment rule should be prescribed for the area that is most problematic: business income taxes. Given that no apportionment rule is truly "correct," since income often has no specific location, the exact content of the rule is unimportant so far as the tax merits are concerned. One particular rule, however—a three-factor formula based on profits, payroll, and sales that counts all three factors equally to connote simplicity and objectivity—might be the most consistent with both current practice and the message that Congress is simply providing a fair and uniform rule, not making a nuanced political or policy judgment. Whatever rule Congress chooses should apply not only to corporate income taxes but also to the income of business entities such as partnerships that are included in the taxable income of individuals.[3]

---

[2]See Hellerstein and Hellerstein, *State and Local Taxation*, pp. 500–505.

[3]A statutory answer to many income allocation issues already exists at the state

Such a rule would not end all controversy over the location of taxable income. Recall, for example, issues such as where baseball teams or phone companies have their profits, payrolls, and sales. A host of industry-specific rules might be warranted, and on these one might expect lobbying and political disagreement. To limit the continuous political input, Congress could direct that industry-specific elaborations of the general rule be developed administratively, as by the Treasury Department, pursuant to the general directive that in all cases exactly 100 percent of a taxpayer's U.S. income should be apportioned to all the states together.

For personal income taxes, questions of business entity income aside, the allocation problems tend to be less serious in practice. When one works and resides in a single state, only that state can impose an income tax under the judicial requirement of nexus. While disparate multiple taxation may arise when a taxpayer resides in one state and works in another, the states generally, although not universally, coordinate their exercise of taxing powers under the Multistate Tax Compact, particularly by providing credits to residents for liability incurred elsewhere.[4] The existing degree of interstate cooperation here—presumably founded on residents' capacity to perceive the double taxation and complain effectively about it—reduces the need for a solution at the national level, but one might still want to require that the compact be followed in all cases.

For sales and use taxes, the relatively high degree of interstate cooperation usually ameliorates coordination problems. Congressional action could again take the form of requiring adherence to the Multistate Tax Compact, thus making universal the "destination" rule for place of sale and the requirement that states provide tax credits for sales or use taxes previously paid to other states.[5] Congress could also require greater uniformity between a state's sale and use taxes so that out-of-state sales would not be disfavored.[6] Perhaps more important, to eliminate what is in effect a tax preference favoring out-

level, in the form of the Uniform Division of Income for Tax Purposes Act, currently subscribed to by twenty-five states and the District of Columbia. See ibid.

[4]See ibid., p. 969.

[5]See ibid., pp. 781–82.

[6]See ibid., p. 783.

of-state purchases, Congress could overturn *National Bellas Hess* and require all out-of-state vendors to collect use taxes and remit them to the taxing jurisdictions.[7]

A further coordination problem worth addressing arises under sales taxes other than those on final retail sales of property—for example, taxes on the sale of services used to produce property for sale or on transfers during production and marketing. Here, multiple taxation occurs unless the sales taxes imposed at earlier stages are credited against those imposed later.[8] The general requirement that retail vendors collect sales and use taxes from purchasers (the *National Bellas Hess* exception aside) should make mandatory crediting feasible.

Property taxes present a similar danger of penalizing multijurisdictional presence under at least two scenarios: one, when they apply to intangible property in one state that is valuable because of the rights it conveys in tangible property in other states and, two, when jurisdiction over the same property is asserted by one state based on the taxpayer's residence or domicile and by another state based on the property's location. Once again, mandatory tax credits would be appropriate,[9] particularly now that the Supreme Court has cast doubt on its willingness to intervene.[10]

---

[7]This has frequently been proposed. See ibid., p. 825. The most prominent proposals exempt vendors with sales (total or within the taxing state) below certain threshold amounts. This creates a tax preference for small business and may inefficiently discourage businesses from crossing the thresholds but is arguably justified on the ground that small vendors' per-sale compliance costs would be disproportionately or even prohibitively high. In North Dakota v. Quill Corp., 112 S. Ct. 1904 (1992), the Supreme Court confirmed that Congress has the power to reverse National Bellas Hess.

[8]See, for example, Mundstock, "Florida Services: You Only Tax Twice?"

[9]Following practice in the personal income tax area, and in keeping with what seems to be the dominant thrust of Schoettle's analysis of tax discrimination, the jurisdiction that should be required to allow a credit for the other jurisdiction's taxes should probably be the one where the taxpayer resides or has his domicile.

[10]See Ford Motor Credit Co. v. Florida Dept. of Revenue, U.S. Sup. Ct., No. 88-1847 (May 20, 1991), where an equally divided Court declined to strike down Florida's intangible property tax that applied both to in-state domiciliaries and to items with an in-state business situs, despite the tax's evident inconsistency with the recently promulgated "internal consistency" requirement. Even if the Supreme Court were clearly willing to act, mandatory crediting would be preferable to its exercise of authority. Since internal consistency is satisfied where liability rests

99

A final proposal concerns the excise or severance taxes that states such as Alaska, Montana, and Wyoming use in an apparent effort to export tax burdens to out-of-state consumers. Such taxes could be constrained, for example, by the requirement that their rates not exceed the taxing jurisdiction's generally applicable sales tax rates, except to the extent demonstrably justified as user fees that recover direct costs to the taxing state specifically resulting from the extraction activity, such as the construction of special roads for mining or expenditures to repair environmental harm. Similar rules could apply to other clear-cut instances of attempted tax exportation, such as hotel taxes.

Prescribed Forms of Tax Bases. A more ambitious set of proposals—plainly defensible under the analysis in this volume but politically less likely—would prescribe the content of entire tax bases. States that levy income taxes could be required to use the federal income tax base, possibly with a small number of specified allowable variations.[11] This requirement would not only reduce opportunities for discrimination against outsiders or interstate commerce but also significantly reduce compliance costs, especially for taxpayers subject to income tax in many jurisdictions. The proposal would generalize a rule of conformity to the federal income tax that many states already follow, at least in part.[12] Even to the extent that the proposal would limit states' discretion, there seems little to regret, for exam-

either on domicile or on business situs, so long as it does not rest on both, problems would arise where states differed in which of the two they employed. Thus, interstate commerce might remain disfavored in practice, subject to the Supreme Court's cumbersome searching for bias in particular cases.

[11]Alternatively, conformity could be required solely for corporate income taxes, since corporations are far more likely to have multijurisdictional presence. A further possible variation would be to condition the federal deductibility of personal state and local income taxes on conformity to the federal base, thus merely encouraging rather than requiring conformity.

[12]As an alternative to federal conformity, Charles McLure has suggested barring states from taxing corporate income, while instead allowing them to tax corporate or all business in-state sales and payrolls. He argues that this would not change the real economic incidence of state corporate income taxes, would make such incidence more widely understood (since many people erroneously regard such taxes as borne by shareholders), and would greatly simplify tax administration. McLure, "The State Corporate Income Tax," pp. 341–42. While this proposal may be meritorious, I ignore it here because of its potentially distracting (even misleading) appearance of reducing progressivity.

100

ple, in ending California's use of its own depreciation system or the differences in carryover periods for capital losses and net operating losses.

One possible objection to the proposal is that it would complicate the fiscal planning of state and local governments. Changes to the federal income tax base would affect state and local tax revenues, and while this procedure calls merely for rate adjustments (assuming a goal of keeping expected revenues constant), in some cases state and local governments might be unable to respond in timely fashion. The Federal Tax Reform Act of 1986, for example, which had dramatic revenue effects on states that voluntarily conform to the federal base, applied to the 1986 taxable year;[13] yet it was not officially enacted until late October of that year, by which time many state legislatures were no longer in session. This problem has a simple solution, however. Either in general or under specified circumstances, states could be required or allowed to provide for a one-year lag in their conformity to the federal income tax base. Given the recent rapidity of federal income tax revision,[14] the federal and state income tax bases might only rarely be identical under this proposal, but at least the number of income tax bases to which any taxpayer was subject would be capped at two.[15]

Among its other applications, a requirement of general income tax conformity would bar states from engaging in worldwide unitary taxation, since that method is not employed for federal income tax purposes. At present, political support for this particular application of the conformity principle appears to be far stronger than support for income tax conformity in general. Legislation has been introduced in both houses of Congress under which the states would be barred from engaging in worldwide unitary taxation.[16]

---

[13]See Hellerstein and Hellerstein, *State and Local Taxation*, p. 937.

[14]See Richard Doernberg and Fred McChesney, "On the Accelerating Rate and Decreasing Durability of Tax Reform," *Minnesota Law Review* 71 (1987): 913.

[15]Requiring conformity to the federal income tax base, with or without a one-year lag, would fail to prevent the states from diverging in their practices of administrative enforcement or in their judicial interpretations of the federal income tax statute, although the latter would be subject to review by the U.S. Supreme Court, given the assumed federal statute requiring conformity. Yet substantial or predominant conformity clearly seems attainable.

[16]On recent legislative consideration of the issue, see Hellerstein and Hellerstein, *State and Local Taxation*, pp. 608–9.

Even without the enactment of a general income tax conformity statute, the proposed legislation barring states from engaging in worldwide unitary taxation appears desirable, given the compliance burdens that such taxation involves and the benefits of nationwide uniformity. The proposed legislation is troubling in only one respect: as a possible precedent for piecemeal intervention by Congress in state and local taxation. Conceivably, in the next case piecemeal intervention could take the form of shrinking state and local tax bases in response to lobbying pressure without regard to the principle of conformity between income tax systems.[17] While lobbying pressures to shrink the tax base may come to bear whenever Congress considers legislation on taxes, at least for provisions that apply to both federal and state or local taxes there is a countervailing cost: reducing federal tax revenues leaves Congress with less money to spend unless it incurs the political cost of raising someone else's taxes, assuming some constraint on deficit spending.

If the dangers of undesirable piecemeal intervention by Congress do not appear too great, several other specific proposals for increasing income tax uniformity might be worth considering, assuming that Congress declines to take the better course of requiring income tax conformity in general. The steps that could be taken—or urged of state legislatures, if congressional action is thought too risky—to reduce the compliance burdens resulting from diversity include the following:

• require the allowance of S corporation elections for state and local income tax purposes whenever they are allowed for federal income tax purposes
• eliminate state-level alternative minimum taxes. By its nature, an alternative minimum tax is a separate tax system, applied in parallel to the regular tax system, and thus in many instances it doubles taxpayers' record-keeping and computational burdens. Depreciable assets, for example, generally have separate bases for

---

[17]Prior isolated interventions by Congress in the state and local tax area have not led to this sort of degradation of the process, however. An example of such intervention is the Railroad Revitalization and Regulatory Reform Act of 1976, Pub. L. No. 94-210, §306, 90 Stat. 31, 54 (1976) (codified at 49 U.S.C. §11503, [barring state and local taxation of railroad property at a higher rate than that generally applicable to commercial and industrial property in the same jurisdiction]).

102

regular tax and alternative minimum tax purposes, given the use of separate depreciation systems. Whatever the merits of the federal alternative minimum tax, imposing such burdens in numerous state jurisdictions is clearly undesirable.[18] States that wished to parallel the reduction in the value of tax preferences that the federal income tax system accomplishes through the alternative minimum tax could rely instead, at a lower compliance cost to taxpayers, on a rule adding back to regular taxable income (subject to apportionment among the states) a percentage of the difference between federal regular and alternative minimum taxable income.

• bar states from applying their own depreciation systems. States could be permitted to require that a portion of federally allowable depreciation deductions be first added back to taxable income and then treated as a separate tax account to be deducted over a longer period. This would simplify record keeping, in comparison with the use of a separate depreciation system, by eliminating the need for taxpayers to keep track of more than one tax basis for each separate asset.

• require the states to adopt the federal income tax carryover periods for tax attributes such as capital losses and net operating losses

• require states to grant income tax filing extensions automatically when extensions are allowed for federal income tax purposes

• require all states to apply a uniform deadline for reporting adjustments to one's federal income tax return

Arguments also could be made for standardizing tax bases other than the income tax. The problem is that Congress may be less trustworthy when it is specifying tax bases that are not being used by the national government. Thus, barring the enactment, say, of a national sales or value-added tax, greater uniformity may best be pursued at the state and local levels (despite its being impeded there by the forces favoring the separate exercise of discretion, to serve either as particular political objectives or as an end in itself).

Steps apart from standardization could also be taken to reduce administrative and compliance burdens, whether or not it is desirable to have Congress enter the field by requiring them. In particular,

---

[18]See Daniel Shaviro, "Perception, Reality, and Strategy: The New Alternative Minimum Tax," *Taxes* 66 (1988): 91.

property taxes would be less burdensome—as well as less subject to discriminatory application—if, instead of being based in many instances on subjective assessments of value, they followed simply from numerical calculations such as historical cost plus a reasonable annual growth factor.[19] Similarly, excise and severance taxes would be less burdensome if they were always volumetric, instead of sometimes employing the netback method based ultimately on contract price. Admittedly, for both types of taxes, state and local reliance on value or contract price has an advantage: it causes tax liability to vary automatically with what might loosely be deemed the taxpayer's ability to pay, whereas the historical cost-based and volumetric methods would require legislative action to adjust for shifts in value. Arguably, however, legislatures that regard this advantage as more significant than the increased burden of value-based taxes, even if they duly consider questions of administrative cost to the state government, are failing to give sufficient weight to the compliance costs taxpayers incur, as well as the danger of discriminatory application in audits.[20]

Intrastate variations in tax rate or base may be comparable in significance to those between states. Thus, while the allocation of authority to local governments is typically considered an issue for the states themselves, not the national government, the national economic consequences of such allocation should not be ignored. Even if the state governments are best situated to respond to problems

---

[19]The Supreme Court recently upheld a property tax valuation formula based on historical cost. Nordlinger v. Hahn, 112 S. Ct. 2326 (1992). The case concerns the so-called "Welcome, Stranger" rule under California's property tax, whereby a property's valuation cannot increase by more than 2 percent per year while it is under the same ownership, but properties are reassessed at the purchase price upon sale to a third party. The asserted problem was the unrealistically low annual inflation factor. In Allegheny Pittsburgh Coal Co. v. County Commn. of Webster County, 488 U.S. 336 (1989), the Court struck down a local "Welcome, Stranger" enforcement policy where it caused eight- to thirty-five-fold disparities in the tax valuations of properties that were worth the same amount, but there the policy was a feature of local administration rather than of the state constitution.

[20]Under ideal conditions, legislatures would take into account taxpayers' compliance costs, because these could be converted dollar for dollar into higher tax liability without prompting additional exit. One reason this trade-off does not always occur may be that the trade-off might not be possible without either overtly discriminating against interstate commerce or raising in-state voters' taxes along with those paid by outsiders.

such as intrastate discrimination against outside business or tax exportation between localities, the problem of administrative and compliance burden, particularly for nationwide businesses, demands national attention. Here the problem is potentially even more serious than at the interstate level, since there is no automatic ceiling on the number of area-specific rules that may arise within states. Fifty states are capable of spawning any number of separate smaller taxing jurisdictions.

As for the sales tax, 7,000 separate jurisdictions are simply too many. The excess would be particularly objectionable if out-of-state vendors were required to collect use taxes under a congressional reversal of *National Bellas Hess* (or changes in Supreme Court doctrine having comparable effect, such as making even more lenient the definitions of *nexus* and *unitary business*). Thus, either in general or as a precondition to compelling out-of-state vendors to remit use taxes, states could be required to cap the number of their separate sales tax jurisdictions. A cap of, say, ten such jurisdictions per state—applied uniformly to all states or on average, with variations in proportion to state population—would reduce more than tenfold the current number of jurisdictions.[21] At present, eighteen states have only one sales tax jurisdiction, and another five have fewer than twenty separate jurisdictions.[22]

Income taxes, property taxes, and various incidental items such as environmental and utility taxes and fees also vary greatly within states in ways that can impose substantial compliance burdens. While greater uniformity is no doubt possible and desirable, a nationally imposed solution is less clearly called for here (except with regard to income taxes, whose bases I have already suggested should conform at the interstate level). It might be unwise to require broader conformity, for two reasons. First, jurisdictions should still be able to control the amount of revenue they raise, a goal that becomes harder to achieve as more taxes are made identical. (This objection

---

[21]Restricting the number of sales tax jurisdictions would require states to revise their methods for dividing revenue among local governments, but this is not necessarily regrettable. Given the arguments for locational neutrality made in this volume, I see no reason to believe that the current regime ranks high in either equity or efficiency.

[22]See Advisory Committee on Intergovernmental Relations, *Significant Features of Fiscal Federalism.*

applies considerably more to the allowance of rate variation than of base variation.) Second, to the extent that provisions (whether or not denominated "taxes") function as user fees—for example, environmental levies for pollution at the site of a factory—they should not be standardized to begin with, since the local circumstances affecting the appropriate amount of the charge may vary.

Choosing Tax Rates Applicable to Different Tax Bases. Even if the states retained only the power to decide what tax rates to apply to federally constrained or prescribed tax bases, locational distortion would persist. By moving toward tax base uniformity, one would hope merely to reduce such distortion, before the costs of uniformity (due to reduced state and local autonomy) begin to outweigh its benefits. One could argue, however, that the proposals I have advanced so far do not go far enough in the direction of limiting discretion.

In particular, if states retain total discretion regarding which of the allowable tax bases they use and what rates to apply to these bases, not only would great variation continue to exist but also some problems of discrimination would be replicated. Consider, for example, Iowa, which, being primarily a market rather than a business state, employs a corporate income tax allocation formula based solely on in-state sales rather than on the standard three factors. Even if that opportunity were eliminated by the imposition of uniform rules governing both allocation and measurement of corporate income, Iowa arguably could still accomplish a measure of perceived or actual tax exportation simply by continuing to rely heavily on the corporate income tax, rather than, say, on property, sales, and personal income taxes that are paid to a greater extent by in-staters.

If state corporate income taxes present the principal remaining tax exportation problem, because out-of-state companies are the most natural deep-pocket targets, a simple solution would be to constrain the rates of such taxes, either absolutely or in relation to the rates of other taxes levied by the same jurisdiction. In favor of such a limitation, one could argue, as Charles McLure does, that state corporate income taxes are unusually unmeritorious. In addition to imposing large compliance burdens, they are perhaps the greatest existing state-level tool of fiscal illusion, largely failing not only to shift costs out of state but even to allocate real tax burdens progressively (presumably one of their principal aims).[23] Given the wide-

---

[23]McLure argues that the real economic incidence of state corporate income taxes

spread belief that corporate income taxes are progressive in incidence, however, a proposal to limit them at the state level might
create political confusion between the issue of federalism in taxation
and the separate issue of tax progressivity.

If state corporate income taxes are just one example of a more
serious problem, or if the problem is best stated in broader terms to
avoid political confusion between the issues of federalism and progressivity, it might be thought desirable to constrain state discretion
further by prescribing outer bounds to the disparities between the tax
rates applied to different tax bases. Among a set of tax bases, such
as personal income, corporate income, sales, and property, for
example, states could be barred from taxing any one base at a rate
more than three times as high, or five percentage points higher, than
the rate applied to any of the other bases.

Yet such a proposal, while not contrary to the analysis in this
book, does not appear necessary. Consider what are probably the
three most critical problems of locational distortion posed by federalism in taxation: administrative and compliance costs, discrimination against outside business, and perceived or actual tax exportation.
The first of these is not addressed by constraining variations in tax
rates. As for the second, so long as all businesses within the taxing
state's market pay tax at the same rate, insiders are not advantaged
relative to outsiders. Thus, a state that applies extremely uneven
rates to different types of taxes does not create competitive distortions
like those resulting, for example, from Iowa's income allocation rule,
which favors wholly in-state firms by increasing the relative taxes
paid by outsiders. Finally, tax exportation, while perhaps not negli-
gible, is ameliorated by limiting discretion over tax bases even if we
do not limit discretion over tax rates. A state that charges a high rate
on a broad-based levy such as a corporate income tax cannot avoid
directly taxing some in-staters as well as outsiders. This side effect
may provide some political protection for outsiders.

In addition to being unnecessary, constraining variations in tax
rates would plainly approach the point where the costs of increased
uniformity begin to exceed the benefits. As discussed previously, the
more visible an issue, the more plausible it is that local control

resembles that of two tax bases that are generally agreed to be regressive: payroll
and sales. See McLure, "The State Corporate Income Tax," p. 341.

107

enhances voter satisfaction, even if that satisfaction is based on illusions about a tax's effect. Issues of what type of tax to use—for example, whether to rely on income taxes or sales taxes for revenue—are more salient than the details of particular tax bases—for example, the system for income tax depreciation.[24] Requiring uniformity only for determining tax bases, and thus not limiting state and local voter sovereignty on issues many voters may actually care about, diminishes serious doubt that more is being gained than lost by moving toward national uniformity.

Constitutional Limitations on Congressional Power. The proposals discussed in this section might, in varying degrees, reduce the autonomy of state and local governments in taxation below the practices of the past two centuries and below what the framers expected and assumed.[25] This point naturally raises the constitutional question of whether Congress is empowered to impose such significant limitations on the states. The central issue is whether Congress's power to restrict state and local taxation, arising under the commerce and supremacy clauses, is in any relevant respect limited.

The answer appears quite clear initially. Numerous Supreme Court cases interpreting the commerce clause, including a handful that specifically concern congressional restrictions on state and local taxation, establish that Congress's power to restrict state and local taxation of interstate commerce is "plenary and all-pervasive, and unrestricted by competing State interests."[26] The only question, therefore, is whether a particular restriction impermissibly reaches purely intrastate activity beyond the reach of the power over interstate commerce.

---

[24]See chapter 4, section entitled "Preserving Broad State and Local Government Autonomy."

[25]See, for example, *Federalist* No. 46.

[26]Hellerstein and Hellerstein, *State and Local Taxation*, p. 329. Compare Hartman, *Federal Limitation on State and Local Taxation*, p. 703: "The power of Congress to regulate interstate commerce seems so complete and paramount in character that Congress may supersede state action even in areas which admittedly are local or intrastate"; Paul F. Mickey and George B. Mickum, III "Congressional Regulation of State Taxation of Interstate Commerce," *North Carolina Law Review* 38 (1960): 119, 122.

Given this question, one still could argue, for example, that, despite the breadth of Congress's commerce clause powers, a rule requiring conformity between state and federal income taxes is unconstitutional as applied to taxpayers not engaged in interstate commerce. In practice, however, the intrastate limitation appears to have little or no significance. Not only is the currently prevailing definition of what constitutes interstate commerce extremely broad, but taxing purely intrastate taxpayers or activities differently from those subject to the congressional power would raise discrimination issues and thus support requiring uniformity between the two.[27] In other areas, Congress's power to regulate purely intrastate activities because of their indirect effects on interstate commerce has long been settled.[28]

One potential complication should be noted, however. Given the long-standing assumption that in our federal system state and local governments will remain active and important within their sphere, an overly sweeping set of federal restrictions might make the Supreme Court sufficiently uneasy to invite the creation of new constitutional principles limiting Congress's preemptive power. In this regard, the short-lived reign of *National League of Cities v. Usery*,[29] decided by the Supreme Court in 1976 and overruled in 1985,[30] is instructive. In *National League of Cities*, the Supreme Court struck down Congress's extension to state employees of minimum wage and maximum hour requirements under the Fair Labor Standards Act. In a plurality opinion, Justice Rehnquist, straining desperately to make something of the rather vague and exhortatory Tenth Amendment,[31] claimed that it "expressly declares the constitutional policy that Congress may not exercise power in a fashion that impairs the States' integrity

---

[27]See, for example, Wickard v. Filburn, 317 U.S. 111 (1942), holding that the commerce clause power supports federal regulation of wheat grown and consumed on the farm of the grower.

[28]See, for example, Houston, E & W Texas Ry. v. United States, 234 U.S. 342 (1914); United States v. Darby, 312 U.S. 100 (1941).

[29]426 U.S. 833 (1976).

[30]Garcia v. San Antonio Metro. Transit Auth., 469 U.S. 528 (1985).

[31]The Tenth Amendment provides: "The powers not delegated to the United States by the Constitution, nor prohibited by it to the States, are reserved to the States respectively, or to the people."

or their ability to function effectively in a federal system."[32]

As a matter of textual interpretation, Chief Justice Rehnquist's account of what the amendment "expressly declares" is extremely weak. The amendment, in its own words, applies only to "powers not delegated to the United States by the Constitution"—to wit, powers other than the commerce clause power at issue in the case. As the expression of a historically rooted constitutional instinct, however, the chief justice's position arguably has more force. Surely one might pause before concluding that, simply because the commerce clause power has been interpreted as virtually universal, Congress has the power to eliminate essentially all state and local government authority. The question, then, is where and on what constitutional ground to draw the line, assuming that such a line should be drawn judicially rather than politically.

In this regard, *National League of Cities* provided little but what one commentator has termed "a variety of inexact and overstated expressions,"[33] relying principally on the notion that Congress may not interfere with states' "integral operations in areas of traditional government functions,"[34] which are not easily defined. In large part, it was the unworkability of this standard that led to reversal of *National League of Cities* in 1985 and to the Supreme Court's conclusion that the states must instead look to the national political process for protection.[35]

Yet *National League of Cities* may not be irreversibly repudiated. Among current members of the Supreme Court, Justices Rehnquist and O'Connor are explicitly committed to the revival of *National League of Cities*.[36] Since the case seems generally to appeal more to conservatives (perhaps because they are more hostile to economically activist national legislation), it is conceivable that Justices Scalia, Kennedy, Souter, and Thomas would consider voting to revive it,

---

[32]National League of Cities, 426 U.S. at 851. Justice Blackmun, concurring and providing the crucial fifth vote for the holding, appeared to suggest balancing federal and state interests case by case. See 426 U.S. at 856.

[33]Hartman, *Federal Limitations on State and Local Taxation*, p. 679.

[34]National League of Cities, 426 U.S. at 852.

[35]See Garcia, 469 U.S. at 539, 546–47, 556.

[36]See 469 U.S. at 580 (Rehnquist, J., dissenting), 589 (O'Connor, J., dissenting).

particularly if Congress acts so aggressively that their confidence in the political check is reduced.[37] As a practical matter, then, there may be outside limits, perhaps more aesthetic than logical, on how far Congress can go in state and local taxation. Still, the proposals that I endorse, which are limited to addressing coordination problems between states' tax systems and to conforming tax bases to reduce burdens on interstate commerce, should be well within any such limits.

In the event that any of the proposals I discuss are held to exceed Congress's constitutional power, or if the judgment is made that states should merely be encouraged, not required, to coordinate their tax systems, Congress could follow a course other than mandating state and local tax rules.[38] It could, for example, make coordination a prerequisite to a particular tax's being deductible for federal income tax purposes—although this might appear to penalize the wrong party if the taxpayer, rather than the state, is assumed to bear the extra burden (and particularly where the taxpayer is from out of state). Or Congress could tie particular categories of federal funding to state and local adherence to appropriate coordination rules.

The Federal Courts

If Congress took sufficient steps to regulate state and local taxation, the main federal judicial role would change from interpreting the Constitution in the context of congressional silence to interpreting federal laws. Thus, even if the courts remained active in reviewing state and local taxes, their views concerning the negative commerce clause would lose significance, given the statutory grounds on which discriminatory taxes would presumably be subject to challenge in most cases. In the absence of substantial congressional action, however, the choice of judicial standard under the negative commerce clause is consequential. I have already suggested that current nega-

---

[37]For Justice Scalia, however, the lack of textual support from the Tenth Amendment and the difficulty of drawing a simple line between permissible and impermissible national legislation might militate against reviving National League of Cities.

[38]Such a judgment could be based on a belief in federalism as a norm even when it is not judicially enforceable, or on the view that states where sentiment is strong enough should be allowed to opt out, or simply on concerns of political feasibility.

tive commerce clause doctrine is seriously deficient, in large because of the Supreme Court's effort to balance a concern about discrimination with a concern for the value of state and local government autonomy. Moreover, I have suggested that such doctrine should single-mindedly focus on harm to outsiders and interstate commerce, instead of attempting to balance it against the value of state and local government autonomy. The principal remaining question is how to conceptualize this change: that is, what the revised judicial standard should look like.

Unfortunately, no one concise test can capture what the courts should do. The problems that may arise, ranging from hostility to outside business competition to attempted tax exportation to disregard for the creation of undue compliance costs, are simply too various. Moreover, the courts' institutional competence to detect these problems and design workable solutions varies significantly with the context. I therefore suggest that the courts invalidate state and local taxes under the negative commerce clause when these taxes violate any of the following tests:

• *Comparative marginal cost test.* As discussed previously, this test has certain shortcomings.[39] Its distinction between fixed and variable costs may be unclear in practice and perhaps is even more unclear in theory. In the long run, all tax costs are variable and influence the structure of interstate markets. Nonetheless, the test is useful, given that not all locational disparities can be struck down consistently within a federal system, because it identifies a class of undesirable tax disparities that state and local political processes may systematically produce. Outsiders are likely to be disfavored by state and local political processes, even where they have potential in-state allies such as consumers.[40] Moreover, Schoettle's distinction between fixed and variable costs is roughly compatible with the insight that basic locational decisions, such as where to reside or locate one's business, are less elastic than decisions to enter a jurisdiction for limited purposes such as the sale of goods, making

---

[39]See chapter 3, section entitled "Attempts to Make the Discrimination Standard Coherent."

[40]See chapter 3, section entitled "Why Bar Discrimination While Permitting Other Locational Disparity?"

them (the realm of his variable costs) more subject to inefficient distortion.[41] The comparative marginal cost test, therefore, is a major advance over current legal doctrine, giving more coherent and concrete economic content to the murky concept of discrimination against interstate commerce.

• *The Supreme Court's internal consistency test.* Under this test, a state or local tax is struck down if its adoption by all jurisdictions would lead to overtaxation of interstate commerce. The value of this test lies in its requiring states to make reasonable efforts at equitable apportionment of the tax base when more than one state has a potential claim, although merely requiring some reasonable effort at apportionment is inferior in principle to mandating consistent apportionment rules that all states will follow.[42] For the courts, however, the simplicity of the application of the internal consistency test is in some situations a decisive advantage. It can eliminate the need for a court either to act like a legislature by mandating specific apportionment rules or to engage in a detailed examination of how different states' apportionment rules interact.

"Rules of the road" or apportionment rules that have attracted widespread consensus among the states. The judicial agnosticism or timidity about prescribing particular allocation rules that underlies the internal consistency test need not always be decisive. When particular allocation rules have attracted widespread consensus among the states, the courts can go beyond internal consistency and require that holdout states accept those rules, in effect, as "rules of the road."[43] Possible applications include requiring adherence to consensus rules regarding which state must be the one to provide a

---

[41]See chapter 3, section entitled "Attempts to Make the Discrimination Standard Coherent."

[42]The internal consistency test does not always succeed in requiring a reasonable effort at apportionment, as Moorman Mfg. Corp. v. Blair, 437 U.S. 267 (1978), makes clear. Iowa's sales-only apportionment rules were in accord with internal consistency.

[43]Past Supreme Court commerce clause cases regarding regulation by state and local governments have treated uniformity as an important value and imposed what were literally rules of the road. See, for example, Kassel v. Consolidated Freightways Corp., 450 U.S. 662 (1981), striking down an Iowa law barring certain large trucks that were allowed on the roads of all neighboring states, partly on the ground that Iowa's divergence from the norm burdened interstate commerce.

tax credit when states' tax bases overlap[44] and the use of a three-factor allocation formula for multistate business income—perhaps (depending on one's tolerance for specific judicial prescription) even adding specificity to the rule of the road by requiring that the three factors be weighted equally.

This test, along with the internal consistency test, could be generalized as an application of a broader principle that states must make some good faith effort at tax base apportionment for multistate activities. A test more generally requiring good faith efforts at apportionment, while worth considering, might create too much uncertainty about judicial outcomes. Assuming that Iowa's single-factor unitary business income apportionment rule is struck down but that no one variant of the three-factor test is mandated, for example, what about the Minnesota rule, which applies to the standard three factors but assigns 70 percent of the weight to sales and only 15 percent each to profits and payroll? If that rule is struck down, what about states that double-weight the sales factor? Perhaps it is best not to give much content to the good faith principle beyond requiring internal consistency and mandating adherence to consensus rules of the road.

Moreover, significant attempted tax exportation should be barred, whether perceived or actual. To detect instances of significant attempted tax exportation, the courts should generally look for two critical identifying features: first, the use of a tax base that disproportionately reaches outsiders, at least in direct incidence or in the short run, and second, the application to that base of a tax rate higher than the rates applied within the jurisdiction to other fiscally significant tax bases. Under a test barring taxes with these two

---

[44]Under state and local personal income taxes, for example, if a resident of one state earns income in another state and both states include such income in their tax bases, the state of residence is generally the one that provides a tax credit for income taxes paid to the other state. See Hellerstein and Hellerstein, *State and Local Taxation*, pp. 968–69. This happens to be the correct place for the credit under the Schoettle test, but it might be worth following as a "rule of the road" even if neither state, more than the other, was the right one to provide a credit. Under another "rule of the road," in the case of an interstate sale that both the seller's and the buyer's jurisdictions subject to sales tax, priority generally goes to the state of destination, and the seller's jurisdiction provides a tax credit. See ibid., pp. 781–82.

114

characteristics, numerous states' excise and severance taxes would probably be struck down (subject to reinstatement at lower rates), as might certain corporate income or other business taxes.

Judicial review based on the above recommendations might be inferior, in both effectiveness and predictability, to a well-designed legislative solution. The well-known institutional disadvantages of using courts to implement broad rules and policies are hard to overcome.[45] Yet the tests should at least make possible the achievement of an ordinary and acceptable level of judicial failure, in comparison with the extraordinary level that has characterized negative commerce clause doctrine from its earliest days until the present. Moreover, in comparison with the alternative of no significant judicial review of state and local taxes, these recommendations should improve at the margin the functioning of our integrated national markets.

---

[45]See, for example, ibid., pp. 324–25.

About the Author

DANIEL SHAVIRO is professor of law at the University of Chicago Law School with a specialty in tax policy and the legislative process, integrating legal, economic, and political science perspectives. His frequent articles have appeared in a number of law reviews and tax policy journals, including the *Harvard Law Review, University of Chicago Law Review, Michigan Law Review, Pennsylvania Law Review*, and *Tax Law Review*. His work emphasizes minimizing the undesirable behavioral effects and compliance costs resulting from taxation and understanding the political, perceptual, and other factors that influence the structure of legal rules in taxation and elsewhere.

Mr. Shaviro received his A.B. summa cum laude from Princeton University in 1978 and his J.D. from Yale Law School in 1981. Before joining the University of Chicago Law School faculty in 1987, he spent three years with the Washington, D.C., law firm of Caplin & Drysdale, Chartered, followed by three years as a legislation attorney to the Joint Committee on Taxation of the U.S. Congress, where he worked extensively on the Tax Reform Act of 1986.